I Ran With

'How can I resist a combo of Martin Knigh
– Irvine Welsh

'It's really good writing, it's a really good s
you can hear Alan on every page. It's ex
taining; there's bits that are really funny,
in it.' – Karin Ingram

Praise for the Bay City Rollers:

'… they were the ORIGINAL boy-b
– *Smooth Radio*

'Arguments over artistic merit may rag
City Rollers were a pop phenomenon. T
Britain, but in the US, Canada, Australi
Scottish acts of the time could dream o
most crafted; unassuming individuals, a
plotted with mathematical precision.' –

'My absolute favourite [band], of cour
they were huge when I was in my te
them… I could tell you every single B
lyric.' – Judy Murray, BBC Radio 4's *I*

'The Bay City Rollers captured the wo
anthems.' – Ken Sharp, *Bay City Bab*
of the Bay City Rollers

'The group were a pop sensation.' –

'For two years, they were the biggest
the USA)' – *The Guardian*

I Ran With The Gang

My Life In and Out of the Bay City Rollers

by founder member
ALAN LONGMUIR

with
Martin Knight

Luath Press Limited
EDINBURGH
www.luath.co.uk

First published 2018

Reprinted 2018

ISBN: 978-1-912147-75-5

The paper used in this book is recyclable. It is made from low chlorine pulps produced in a low energy, low emission manner from renewable forests.

Printed and bound by TJ International, Padstow

Typeset in 11 point Sabon by Lapiz

I dedicate this book to my beloved wife and soulmate, Eileen.

She picked me up when I was down and has put up with me ever since.

Also, to Neil Porteous. He was the third Roller, my cousin and best friend. I miss him every day.

'These wee boys should have had everything'

– Bill Martin

Contents

8

Acknowledgements

THIS BOOK IS the story of my life as I best remember it, in and out of the Bay City Rollers. I will not be dishing dirt, speculating, commenting or making any shocking revelations about the personal lives of any of my band colleagues. What happened or didn't happen to them is their business and not for me to state or judge. They can, have and might write their own accounts. In this book I will willingly invade my own privacy, but not theirs.

I apologise in advance to anybody whose part in my story I have overlooked or forgotten. My recall is not so great these days, which is one of the reasons why I decided to write down my memoirs.

I would like to thank my family for their support, not only in this endeavour but in everything in my life. Also, my circle of friends – some old, some new. I am really very lucky on that score.

Finally, I would like to thank and send love to the fans. Without you none of this would have been possible and you are as much a part of this extraordinary adventure as anybody.

Alan Longmuir
June 2018

I WOULD LIKE to thank Jim Grant for introducing me to Alan; to Alan's close pals Alastair Muir and Chris Balanowski, not only did they supply a car and house, respectively, for our use they created an ambient atmosphere for Alan to recall stories from his life; Debra Blakley for providing all manner of Roller material and memorabilia, and a deep knowledge of the band's history; Derek Longmuir, Alan's brother and bandmate, and Sandra Young, Alan's cousin, for information on their family and the band's background. Thanks are due to Janet Gill for sharing her research on Alan's ancestry. And thanks also for the permission to reprint the *Melody Maker* interview, copyright Caroline Coon, and for the permission received from Bill Martin to reproduce lyrics from *Remember*, copyright Martin/Coulter. Most of all I would like to thank Alan Longmuir for his friendship. One of the nicest, humblest men I have ever known.

I would like to dedicate this book to my friend, Mitch Harrison, who died in 2018 while Alan and I wrote the book. Mitch and I made poor attempts together to travel the world at a time when the Bay City Rollers were conquering it.

Martin Knight
October 2018

Foreword
by Martin Knight

I WAS SITTING in a bar in El Campello, a quiet resort on the Costa Blanca somewhere between Alicante and Benidorm, with my wife, daughter, son-in-law and newly arrived grandson, Harry. We were having a beer and a bite to eat, watching the world go by and the blue sea rolling back and forth. A couple were sitting behind us and I could tell by their accents they were Scottish. Somehow, as they sometimes do in outdoor bars and restaurants, our conversations merged into each other. The subject was football. The couple, who introduced themselves as Jim and Shirley Grant, mentioned Dave Mackay, legendary defender of Hearts, Spurs and Derby.

'He wrote his book,' said Ryan, my son-in-law, pointing at me.

'Never. Bloody genius, Dave was. What was he like? Hard bastard, Dave,' said Jim.

The conversation moved on from Scottish football to books and what or who was I writing now. Nothing, I told Jim. But who would you like to write? I don't know. No more footballers. Maybe a rock star. Who? Ringo Starr, I said. He's the only Beatle not to have had a biography or autobiography. Jim countered quickly – what about the Bay City Rollers? 'What about them?' was my first reaction but I didn't verbalise it. I tried to find a path politely away. It crossed my mind for a minute Jim was a Roller himself.

'It's been done, surely?'

'Nae, not really. Alan Longmuir, the founder member, is my mate. He wants to do a book. Bloody coincidence this. Well, do you wannae do it or not?'

I said something non-committal like I'd certainly be interested to find out more and do a bit of research. Jim was a determined man. He took my email and phone number but as we waved goodbye and headed back to our hire car I fully expected never to hear from him again. Another blurred, drink-smeared conversation in a bar. We've all had them.

Maybe a month later, back at home, a number I did not recognise flashed up on my phone. I nearly ignored it thinking it would be likely be an Indian man from a Bangalore call centre informing me in a surreal Yorkshire accent about the latest road collision I had been involved in yet had no memory of.

'Hello?'

'Hello, Martin. Alan Longmuir,' and, in case I didn't know, 'Alan Longmuir. I was in the Bay City Rollers.'

His humble, modest approach set the tone of our subsequent conversations.

I believe my less than enthusiastic response to Jim's initial overture is one that would be shared by many men of my generation, especially in England. We were conditioned to dislike and dismiss the Bay City Rollers at the time and later as history paraded them as the negative poster boys of that much maligned decade – the 1970s.

Of course, I could recall some of their songs. *Bye Bye Baby* particularly. They had a way of embedding themselves in your subconscious. I remembered their individual names, but, besides Les McKeown, I couldn't have told you which one was which such was my detachment. I knew there was one that played guitar who seemed a tad uncomfortable in his tartan-edged trousers riding up his leg. Possibly older than the others he claimed the background, an amused and bemused smile playing on his lips. Like he couldn't quite process what was happening to him and around him. I now know that member was Alan Longmuir.

The Bay City Rollers arrived decisively in the public consciousness at a time of intense musical snobbery. It was the mid-1970s and the country was in a serious mess – quite literally – as rubbish piled up on the streets following industrial action by public sector workers. There were power-cuts and three-day weeks, high unemployment and plummeting stock markets. Denis Healey, the Chancellor, took his begging bowl to the International Monetary Fund to keep the country afloat and The Wombles dominated the singles chart. Yes, depressing times. It says it all that the term 'womble' has entered the English language, permanently, denoting a person who is a complete idiot. It was this timing that accounts for both the Bay City Rollers' enormous impact and their vicious public denigration in some quarters.

In 1967 the album *Sgt. Pepper's Lonely Hearts Club Band* was released, and it marked The Beatles' transformation from the world's most successful pop group to something altogether more serious. Deeper. No longer were the kids twisting. They were sitting cross-legged thinking. Analysing lyrics. Searching for hidden messages. The unseemly scrabble to the higher plane was on.

Musical artists had to act fast and decisively to adapt. Gravitas credentials were demanded. Concept albums were *de rigueur*, greatest hits and foot tappers were passé. Music that did not pass the 'meaningful' test was dismissed and labelled as 'bubble gum' or 'teenybopper'. This was to forget that pop music was traditionally aimed at and created by teenyboppers for teenyboppers. Perfectly good groups like The Searchers, Herman's Hermits and the Dave Clark Five couldn't get a hit for love nor money.

As the 1960s gave way to the 1970s this trend built in momentum. The new musical mindset was termed 'progressive', 'underground' or 'heavy'. Schoolboys risked losing all credibility if they admitted to buying *Chirpy Chirpy Cheep Cheep* by Middle of the Road, although many of them must have as it was number one for five weeks. Youths would carry around copies of the *Tarkus* LP by Emerson, Lake & Palmer under their arms. It was as much a personal and fashion statement as the Afghan coat they were wearing. The reality was when they relaxed in the privacy of their own bedrooms alone they'd probably be playing *The Pushbike Song* by The Mixtures or *Tiger Feet* by Mud rather than subjecting themselves to *Tarkus*.

The 'serious' acts themselves were generally a morose bunch, brooding, with long lank hair in ankle length dull trench coats, preferably pictured staring vacantly into the middle distance. They were producing self-indulgent, sleep-inducing double-albums and taking the view that people who didn't like the 'tracks' didn't understand them. If you didn't dig the music man that was your fault, not theirs.

But adolescent girls did not fall for such nonsense. While all this was being played out they were still buying pop songs with catchy tunes by the truck load and anointing idols like The Osmonds, T. Rex, Slade, David Cassidy and Michael Jackson. They were enjoying the pop scene as they always had. Many boys looked on enviously, yearning for the music they *actually* liked rather than the music they thought they *should* like.

The kickback against the 'heavy' movement that gathered pace from 1971 onwards was soon being labelled 'glam rock'. At various times it was spearheaded by Sweet, Gary Glitter, Alvin Stardust, T. Rex, David Bowie, Slade, Suzi Quatro, Mud and others. The musicians sang and dressed loud, all having their own quirky characteristics and styles. Initially the music intellectuals sneered but even they found it hard to dismantle artists whose talents, charisma and marketability were undeniable. By 1973/4 it was the likes of Emerson, Lake & Palmer, and their ilk, that were looking tired and marginal.

And then came the Bay City Rollers. They had a brief chart flirtation in 1971 but then returned to relative obscurity until 1974 when they assaulted the charts with a string of feel-good, bouncy songs and a look that delighted and infuriated in equal numbers. In tartan-edged trouser-suits, jackets, colourful socks and stack shoes their smiling cherubic faces sent teenage girls into apoplexy and nearly everyone else into a simmering rage. Here was a group of boys that were happy and enjoying themselves. How very dare they? Their name smacked of a band that was trying to ride that American skateboard/surfboard vibe and then it was discovered they were Scottish. Not even English! Out of bloody order!

All the resentment against glam rock, bubble gum, pop, teenybopper could now be marshalled against one entity. Bolan, Noddy Holder, Bowie et al were capable of defending themselves. Their body of work and performance spoke for itself. They were proving themselves in the wider genre. But the Bay City Rollers were easy prey and all the prejudices and vitriol was gathered up and directed against them. It was cultural bullying. The mantra went something like this: *They don't write their own songs/They don't even play their own instruments/Their songs are shit anyway/They look like pratts/They're Scottish/They're manufactured.*

I can remember hearing such abuse about The Monkees a few years before and would hear it again about boy bands and various X Factor creations in the future.

But the Rollers could not easily be dismissed and consigned to the embarrassing shelf in the local record shop. The fan reaction was the closest anyone had come to Beatlemania, surpassing the Monkees, The Osmonds, David Cassidy and artists yet to come including, most notably, Take That and One Direction. It defied logic for many but it was happening. It happened. The Rollers had four or five intense years at the pinnacle, more than the Monkees, The Osmonds and Cassidy and they conquered the world, notably successful in America, Canada, Japan and Australia. In the annals of pop music, they confounded everyone. None of the likes of Slade, T. Rex, Sweet or Gary Glitter had made significant inroads stateside.

The Bay City Rollers are thought to have sold more than 120 million records, probably more. Nobody really knows as the lack of visible accounting is one of the features of the miserable financial backdrop to this story. It is estimated they generated £5bn of revenue at current prices when merchandise sales are included. There was a period when most of the country's teenage girls were wearing something Roller related. There were magazines and annuals, pencil cases and bags. The Rollers image rights should have generated many millions and they certainly did for some people.

History has re-evaluated glam rock and now Sweet, for example, are remembered fondly and with respect, though they were often mocked and denigrated during their pomp. *Crazy Horses*, a song penned and performed by The Osmonds, is today lauded as a pioneering heavy metal classic and David Bowie went on to become one of the most revered and creative artists in the world and in history. Yet the Bay City Rollers remain largely un-re-habilitated. Joey Ramone, Courtney Love and other 'credible' rock figures have come out of the closet and admitted to loving and being influenced by them, but they still attract opprobrium among many.

The proof is in the pudding though. Watch at any wedding or party when the DJ puts on *Bye Bye Baby*. Smiles spread across creased faces, especially the women, and there is a dignified rush to the dance floor. When the Rollers reformed briefly in 2015, two dates at the Hammersmith Apollo were sold out in minutes – likewise, in Barrowlands in Glasgow and other prominent venues. This was 43 years on from their peak and nearly 40 years since they last rode high in the UK charts. More people are fond of the Bay City Rollers and the era and emotions they evoke than is popularly imagined. They just don't admit it, yet.

The irony in all this rock snobbery is that the Rollers *were* from the streets. They'd grown up the hard way in tenement blocks in Edinburgh's poorer districts. No London School of Economics, art school or Charter-house educations among them. They'd served long and arduous apprentice-ships in working men's clubs and dives up and down the British Isles and were competent musicians and accomplished performers. In Les McKeown they had a front-man potentially more wild, working-class and controversial than the so-called bad boys of rock. He was 'proper street'. He was accused of firing an air gun at and injuring a fan. He was involved in a fatal car accident. He fought other band members on stage. Had he died young, the Rollers would have been viewed in a whole different light. Manager Tam Paton may have seen it as a good career move but for Les that would have been a high price to pay have history treat him with respect. Alan Longmuir once wryly observed when the Rollers were attempting a comeback: 'The problem we have is that we're too old to die young.'

Another irony that occurred to me in discovering their back catalogue as part of my research is that, as their popularity waned, their music got better. As Alan's story will tell, they were thwarted by everyone they worked with in trying to grow creatively, although he is the first to admit they would probably have never broken through if they had recorded their own material from the beginning. The more the critics decried them the more the band wanted to prove to the world that they could grow artistically. This battle for credibility eventually contributed to their demise. Some of the tracks from their later albums are mature and strong songs that stand the test of time. *Don't Let The Music Die*, written by Eric Faulkner and Stuart Wood and recorded in 1977, is, in my opinion, one of the best Rollers' efforts and up there with the top ballads by anyone that came out of that decade. If the band had been given the opportunity to have the recording of their own material managed sensibly, I believe they would have enjoyed a much longer career at the top. Bill Martin, who with Phil Coulter co-wrote *Shang-A-Lang*, among others, for the group, has said similar in recent years.

The band's legacy has also been smeared by the nefarious activities of their controlling and dominant manager Tam Paton. It transpired after the boys and he had parted company that he was a predatory paedophile and a major drug dealer among other things. There is a growing suspicion that he may have been an integral part of an organised group who exploited vulnerable children for sexual gratification – the full truth about him has yet to be unearthed. A thoroughly nasty piece of work and now dead, Paton casts an unwelcome shadow over the group. That shadow should evoke sympathy for the Rollers, not otherwise, as they were mere boys, innocents, some as young as 16, when they came under his malign stewardship.

* * *

When I met Alan, he took me to his local pub in Bannockburn. He was quite clearly a regular.

'All right, Shang-a-Lang?'

'That's my nickname in here,' Alan explained sheepishly.

His mate asks me if I can understand his accent. I said I could.

'Strange, I have friends in London and my nickname down there is Subtitles. They can't understand a word I say.'

They are a seasoned and humorous bunch. Alan melts in to the background, his Roller status not counting for much in here. I expect he wouldn't have it any other way. He doesn't look like a former pop star. He looks like a former plumber, which, incidentally, he is. He acknowledges that these days the Rollers attract attention mainly in relation to legal battles, tales of hardship and acrimony, and the Paton factor. He acknowledges a dark side to the Bay City Rollers has emerged and grown in momentum. Alan says he hopes to provide some balance and tell *his* story. After all, he was there at the beginning and at the end: a story of a boy from Dalry who played some guitar and wanted to be famous. He wants to tell of the soaring rollercoaster success, the laughs, the wave of happiness that spread across the globe and the highs and the lows. He doesn't want to settle scores or point fingers. He just wants to get it all out before it's too late. A rags to riches and back again tale with bells on. I get it. We go in the back room and I switch my tape recorder on.

Introduction

by Alwyn Turner

I wish it could be 1975 again

'GOODBYE, GREAT BRITAIN. It was nice knowing you.' The sentiments of the *Wall Street Journal* in 1975 rang all too true for many British people in that difficult year. It was less than ten years since *Time* magazine had anointed London as 'The Swinging City', and so much seemed to have gone wrong in the interim.

Even the emblems of the Swinging Sixties were looking tattered, having barely survived the end of that already-hallowed decade. Mods had become skinheads; the image of Bobby Moore holding aloft the World Cup was tainted by footage of rampaging hooligans; films like *Performance* and *Get Carter* depicted a grubby gangster-ridden world of pornography where once there had been a sexual revolution. And, as a symbolic full stop, Biba – the shop that had set so much of the look of the previous decade – closed down in August 1975, the victim of an unsustainable property boom and crash. 'It really is the end of a dream,' noted cabinet minister Tony Benn, as he walked past the store, unconsciously echoing John Lennon's lyric on the demise of The Beatles: 'The dream is over.'

A tetchy, grumbling note of conflict had entered the culture. By 1975 the nation's favourite TV sitcom was *Love Thy Neighbour*, with Jack Smethurst and Rudolph Walker hurling racial abuse at each other, and the biggest drama series – debuting that year – was *The Sweeney*, depicting the police as boozing, womanising brawlers, almost indistinguishable from the villains they were chasing.

On a bigger stage, there was an unmistakeable note of crisis to be heard, as well, maybe even one of panic. Inflation was creeping towards 30 per cent in the summer of 1975, prompting talk of Weimar Germany and the death of democracy. Retired military officers were proposing the formation of private armies, and dropping dark hints of coups to come, while Northern Ireland was already in the grip of something approaching civil war. The country was still reeling from the political chaos of the previous year, when an oil crisis and a miners' strike had resulted in a state of emergency, two general elections and a three-day working week; there had been food shortages, power-cuts and early closedowns on TV (which was still more likely to be viewed in black-and-white than in colour).

It was Britain's turn to be 'the sick man of Europe', a term first used to describe the Ottoman Empire at the time of the Crimean War and subsequently applied to... well, to pretty much every country on the continent at one point or another. The fact that Britain was neither the first nor the last sick man was little comfort, though. Not when the phrase was coupled with another: 'the British disease', referring to the terrible state of industrial relations.

The country was, in short, experiencing a harsh comedown from the adrenalin rush of the sixties. Perhaps it was inevitable. The rapid collapse of the world's largest ever empire, in the space of a single generation, had led to a confusion of identity, an uncertainty over the nature of what Britain had become. While the extraordinary boom in popular culture – the worldwide success of James Bond and The Beatles, of Michael Caine and Mary Quant – had briefly masked the reality of that predicament, still that uncertainty remained.

It wasn't all doom and gloom, of course; and, even when it was, the doom and gloom were shared out pretty fairly. When there was a power-cut, everyone's lights went out; when the motorway speed limit was reduced to 50 mph to save fuel, all drivers were affected; when an IRA bomb exploded in London, it didn't discriminate between its victims. If the country sometimes felt as if it were under siege conditions, there was at least communality, the reassurance of a shared suffering. While the politicians spoke of the Hungry Thirties, the popular culture was awash with a sense of community that consciously evoked the Blitz spirit. There was a plotline familiar to television viewers of their favourite characters being stranded away from their homes and keeping their spirits up by singing old wartime songs together: it turned up in *Coronation Street*, *Are You Being Served?*, *Mind Your Language* and elsewhere. Although 1975 was the year that a referendum confirmed Britain's membership of what was then the European Community, seeming to suggest a new vision of the country's future, Europe was still seen through the prism of 1940.

These were confusing, confused times.

In addition, rock 'n' roll, which had largely driven the cultural explosion, was enduring its own crisis of identity, apparent at the very dawn of the new decade. In January 1970 The Beatles recorded their last song together,

George Harrison's *I, Me, Mine* (albeit in the absence of John Lennon), and then went their separate ways. In the same month Pink Floyd announced that they would be releasing no more singles, such things being below the dignity of serious musicians. Led Zeppelin, whose second album was then at number one in the American charts (and would shortly reach the top in Britain, displacing *Abbey Road*) never did release a single in Britain. A seemingly unbridgeable gap had opened between rock and pop. The cross-class, cross-gender cultural coalition that had proved so productive in the sixties lay in fragments.

By the end of the year, there was the first sign of an attempt to build a new consensus. T. Rex's *Ride a White Swan* prefigured the rise of glam rock, which took over the charts from 1972. Glam was a style, an attitude, rather than a movement, defined – insofar as it was ever properly defined – by its approach to performance. It was also a broad church, finding room for acts as diverse as Roxy Music and Sweet, or David Bowie and Alvin Stardust.

There was, though, at least one common factor: a vein of nostalgia that ran right through glam. The way forward was to reconnect with the original spirit of rock 'n' roll. The imagery of the 1950s became a touchstone for the songs of the early 1970s: from David Essex's *Rock On* and Gary Glitter's *Rock 'n' Roll (Part One)* to David Bowie's *Rock 'n' Roll Suicide* and Mott the Hoople's *The Golden Age of Rock 'n' Roll*. The early repertoire also returned in a new guise: T. Rex covered Eddie Cochran, Eno covered Neil Sedaka, Suzi Quatro covered Elvis Presley. The same desire to find inspiration in the music of an earlier, more innocent age could be seen on both sides of the Atlantic, with the stage musical *Grease* (1972), the movies *American Graffiti* and *That'll Be the Day* (both 1973), and the TV sitcom *Happy Days* (1974).

This was of a piece with the wider cultural mood. If the present felt like the country was sinking into oblivion, then perhaps the best option was a retreat into the past. Much of the most successful culture of the 1970s was rooted in bygone times: *Upstairs Downstairs, All Creatures Great and Small, Pennies from Heaven*, Laura Ashley, Portmeirion Pottery's Botanic Garden range, *The Country Diary of an Edwardian Lady*, as well as, inevitably, the presence of the Second World War in everything from *Dad's Army* to *Colditz*. Glam was part of that trend, with the crucial difference that rock 'n' roll had just a two-decade history on which to draw.

Glam died as a potent artistic force in the late summer of 1974. Partly its demise was due to the ever-changing tastes of the audience and the industry, but there were two very specific factors at work as well. First, there was the distaste felt by the weightier figures that they were being lumped in with pure pop acts: David Bowie and Roxy Music, in particular, shed their satin and tat and embraced the new sounds of soul. And second, there was a technicians' strike at the BBC, which stopped the making of new shows. One of those hit was *Top of the Pops*, which had become the home of glam, and which was not broadcast for a full month. The result was that new releases by established stars – Suzi Quatro, Mott the Hoople, Wizzard, David Essex – failed to sell anywhere near as well as would normally be the case, and instead there was a rise in music that was primarily to be heard elsewhere, most notably disco, though there was also a return of reggae to the charts.

What glam left behind was a love of dressing up and an appetite for nostalgia. The chart groups who stepped into the newly vacated platform boots were those wearing identifiable uniforms, playing music that was rooted in pre-Beatles pop: Showaddywaddy, Mud, the Rubettes, Kenny. And then, above all, there were the Bay City Rollers.

Because the reason we started in 1975 is that, despite the problems that were wracking the country that year, despite all the crises and the negativity, this was also the Year of the Rollers. By the spring of 1975, they were everywhere: on television with *Shang-a-Lang*, on the cover of every tabloid and every self-respecting teen magazine in the land, and at No.1 with both their album *Once Upon a Star* and their single *Bye Bye Baby*.

That song, of course, was a cover of an old number by the Four Seasons, just as the band's first hit had been a cover of the Gentrys' *Keep on Dancing*. The records in between, the string of hits in 1974 that heralded Rollermania, weren't oldies, but they weren't far off. *Remember (Sha-La-La-La)*, *Shang-a-Lang*, *Summerlove Sensation* – these were songs that deliberately conjured up a bygone era of American pop, a time when the music was simple and direct, and when drugs and politics had yet to manifest themselves. They were nostalgic snapshots of cherished teen summers, remembering the days when the band began to play and we all began to sway – those of us, at least, who were all in the news with our blue suede shoes.

This was slightly odd because these were records aimed at an audience for whom nostalgia was not an option. When the glam acts had referenced the early days of rock 'n' roll, it had made some sense; certainly, it had made sense for the artists themselves, all of whom remembered those times, and some of whom (Alex Harvey, Alvin Stardust, Gary Glitter) had been releasing records back then. But for Rollers fans, there wasn't a great deal to remember. Nor was there, for most, anything much to escape from: strikes by miners or power-workers might damage the economy and disrupt the lives of adults, but for kids they also meant there'd be power-cuts, which were fun because you could have candles at breakfast-time.

In any event, the lyrics to a song like *Shang-a-Lang* didn't matter a great deal, any more than they did in *Bye Bye Baby*, with its inappropriately bouncy tale of adultery. The words were simply the right noises, a collage of half-familiar pop phrases, set to chord sequences that were taken from basic blueprints. This wasn't a re-creation or a revival; more like the distilled essence of pop music's joyous rush. And, as such, it had nostalgia built into its every bar, for while the best pop celebrates the present, it also has a bittersweet subtext that these happy days will never be here again. The nostalgia has survived; heard now, those Rollers' hits are more of their time than almost anything by their contemporaries.

This was another paradox of the 1970s. The state of the nation produced an appetite for an evocation of the past, which proved so powerful that it was adopted as the soundtrack for those too young to have known that past. Now the same music evokes its own era – an era when there was a shared culture, when there was such a thing as society. For those who were there, even if they disparaged the Rollers – and many did – *Bye Bye Baby* is a fast-track ticket back to 1975. And the memories it conjures up are likely to be happier than the newspaper headlines of the time would suggest.

The image of the Bay City Rollers is an indelible stamp on the era: a youth-club gang of a rock 'n' roll band, a blur of big hair, short trousers and skinny chests. And there, off to one side of the stage in the long tradition of semi-detached bassists, was Alan Longmuir. Older than the others – let alone the fans – he was the big brother not only of Derek, but of the whole Rollers family, and he looked on, slightly bemused as it seemed, at the screaming mass of tartan-clad kids behind flimsy security barriers. He gave the appearance of someone not quite able to believe the juvenile juggernaut he'd set in motion.

Alwyn W Turner is a cultural and political historian. His critically acclaimed book Crisis? What Crisis?: Britain in the 1970s *was published in 2008, followed by* Rejoice! Rejoice!: Britain in the 1980s *and* A Classless Society: Britain in the 1990s *in 2010.*

I

Rock 'n' Roll Love Letter

'DEREK.'

'Yes, Alan.'

'Do you want to join my group?'

Derek did not look away from the television. He loved *Bonanza*.

'Your group of what, Alan?'

'My pop group, Derek. Like The Beatles.'

The word 'band' for a pop group hadn't entered common parlance yet. It was the mid-1960s and it was all beat groups and combos. The mention of the word Beatles prompted Derek to turn around and pay attention. The four lads from Liverpool were having that effect on everyone.

'Yes, please.'

'Guid. Now what instrument would you like to play?'

That foxed Derek.

'Well, I'm playing bass guitar because I'm left-handed like Paul McCartney,' I informed my younger brother.

'But you cannae play guitar.'

'Not yet, Derek. Not yet.'

'In that case I'll play drums like Ringo Starr.'

'That's fine. We just need to get some instruments and think of a name.'

'But who will be our John and George?'

I wasn't ready for that. Pondered for a few seconds.

'What's cousin Neil up to these days?'

Aye, it may not have happened quite that way, but the scenario would not be far off the mark. Brother Derek was (and still is) almost three years younger than me – it could have been him courting me. That precise defining moment is lost in the sands of time.

I'd had it in my head to be a pop star for some years even before the loose idea of forming a band first bubbled up inside me. The trigger was going to see a film called *Jailhouse Rock* at the local cinema, The Scotia, in 1958. I was ten-years-old and the star of the film, Elvis Presley, knocked me sideways and awakened all sorts of feelings inside, some of which I could not understand. The plot about a young man in prison who is taught to sing and perform by a fellow jailbird and on release becomes a star was attractive enough in a rebellious and rags to riches way, but the scene where Elvis performs the title track was electrifying. There he was pole dancing four decades before it became popular in nightclubs across Europe. With his thumbs defiantly hitched into his trousers he swivelled, swerved and gyrated. I was too young to understand any nuances in the lyrics but knew I was experiencing a sort of epiphany.

Not as much, though, as the people around me. Teenagers. It was the buzz label. You heard grown-ups talking about them all the time. You read newspapers screaming headlines about them. Television and film analysed them. Anyone would have thought there had been no teenagers until the mid-1950s and, in a way, there hadn't. If you didn't know better you could have thought they had arrived in space ships and were colonising communities with their damned youth clubs, loud records and outlandish clothes. Now I was witnessing teenagers first-hand. They were dancing in the aisles. Boys and girls. Rock 'n' roll dancing. Twirling and spinning each other around. Younger lassies were gripping their seats, kicking their legs wildly, yelping and sighing. Even surly Teddy Boys at the back with their Brylcreemed quiffs, drainpipe trousers and winkle-picker shoes dragged on their cigarettes more urgently, deeply anxious not to reveal any signs that Elvis was impacting on them. As they say, the place was rocking.

I was a great patron of the local cinemas. Films, especially American ones, were our chief source of entertainment. Mum took me to see *Seven Brides for Seven Brothers* when I was very young, but I think the first film I saw was *Annie Get Your Gun* with Doris Day. We loved Doris, us Longmuirs. Also, there was Saturday morning pictures, a collection of short films put together for the kids and to take them off the parents' hands for a couple of hours. I gulped down my weekly ration of Flash Gordon, Buck Rogers, Hopalong Cassidy and the Three Stooges. There might have been some misbehaviour among us kids then. It was not unknown to lob chewed bubble gum across the aisles and shout out rude words at the screen and crawl along the floor between the seats on all fours among the debris to annoy others, but this universal crackling energy I was witnessing with Elvis was something else. I wanted some of that.

I was more excited by the impact than the music. I didn't rush off and buy all of Elvis's records. Nor did I seek out the composers, Jerry Leiber and Mike Stoller, who went on to pen many songs of quality as diverse as *Stand by Me* and *Pearl's a Singer* made their own by Ben E King and Elkie Brooks, respectively. I just wanted to have the stage power of Elvis. Be able to create a stir. Be part of a musical phenomenon.

We had a piano in the house which Dad played, and I slowly taught myself. Have you heard my *Chopsticks*? Dad was also a competent accordionist and I, again, coached myself on that. The accordion is an underrated instrument that is not as easy to play as most people imagine. Auntie Edie was the most talented musically in the extended family and could play our piano well. Edie and her husband Jim Porteous, and their children Neil and Sandra all lived with us for a while just after the war. We had musical evenings around ours or we'd sometimes decamp to a neighbour's. It was really like that then, families in and out of each other's houses. That sort of society has been lost, sadly.

I also sang a bit. When I was 15, I appeared with the Tynecastle School Choir at the Usher Hall, Edinburgh. Sometimes we made a little stage at 5, Caledonian Road, our home, and Derek, my cousin Neil Porteous and I would perform for the adults; maybe recite a poem or sing a little song. Occasionally, I'd don my father's undertaker's top hat to charm the audience. Arguably, these musical interludes were the first performances of the Bay City Rollers. One time I remember, during one of these shows, was when a small packet fell out of Neil's pocket. He had been to the barber shop earlier and pinched a packet of condoms thinking, probably, they were sweets. I knew what they were, but poor old Neil didn't grasp why the adults seemed so embarrassed by it. Afterwards I spent some time explaining (or trying) to Neil what a Rubber Johnny was.

But, I was essentially a shy boy and deep down, although I was bewitched by Elvis Presley in *Jailhouse Rock,* I knew I could never be him. I could never be the front man. The thought of appearing on a stage alone in front of halls full of expectant people terrified me more than it excited me. In fact, the thought of appearing in front of a garden shed full of strangers terrified me more than it excited me. My ambitions to pop stardom went on the back-burner.

The Beatles changed all that. There was a hiatus between Elvis and The Beatles. There was plenty of music around in that five-year period between the coming of Elvis in my life and the birth of the 'Fab Four' but nobody that really tilted the world on its axis. This is not to detract from Billy Fury, Cliff Richard, The Shadows and countless other groups and solo artists. Some of them were exciting but Elvis was a hard act to follow. And none of the British talent had ever broken America. Yet.

John, Paul, George and Ringo first troubled the UK charts late in 1962 with *Love Me Do*. It was a wee hit, peaking at number 17, but it was merely feeling the way for the avalanche to follow. The Beatles already had a massive and passionate following in their home town of Liverpool and were a tight outfit having honed their stagecraft over a few hard graft years at home and in the fleshpots of Hamburg, Germany. Unusually, for the time, they were also writing their own material.

I cottoned on to them in 1963. Their music was everywhere. Fresh, urgent and distinctive pop numbers like *She Loves You* and *I Want to Hold Your Hand*. Rockers like *Twist and Shout*. Ballads like *Yesterday*. Their B sides were better than most other acts' A sides. They were there whenever you switched on the television – on the panel on *Juke Box Jury*, waving on the revolving stage on *Sunday Night at the London Palladium*, even wisecracking with Morecambe and Wise. They were funny, sharp and relaxed. Four working-class laddies who had taken over the world.

Paul McCartney captivated me. Left-handed bassists were few and far between, but he was so much more. He had a great voice that could move quickly from sweet and melodic to earthy and rocky. He was good looking in a next-door-neighbour kind of way. Even in those early days you could see he was diplomatic and determined. And he co-wrote the songs. He and John Lennon were so prolific they were giving them away: *I Wanna Be Your Man* to the Rolling Stones, *Misery* to Kenny Lynch, *Do You Want to Know a Secret* to Billy J. Kramer. The list is endless.

The mainstream could not ignore The Beatles. Newsreels and television showed the fans at their concerts, screaming like we'd never seen before and fainting and throwing themselves recklessly at their idols. Not even Elvis produced mass hysteria on this scale. When they climbed on to their USA bound airplane for the first time at London Airport in early 1964 fans filled the balconies waving and swaying with hundreds locked outside. When they landed at Kennedy Airport it was the same. They'd conquered America from the sky. Until that point we, in the United Kingdom, were all in thrall to American culture: Charlie Chaplin, Fred Astaire, Ginger Rogers, Humphrey Bogart, Laurel and Hardy, Marilyn Monroe, Frank Sinatra and Elvis. Everything the Americans did was better than us in the UK. They lived in smarter, bigger houses. They had refrigerators, we had larders. They cruised around in Buicks, we still pedalled around on Raleigh bicycles. But now we had something they didn't – The Beatles. The Fab Four. They spread across the world like a bushfire. A word was needed to describe what was happening and someone coined the term 'Beatlemania'.

On 29 April 1964, very soon after they returned from that first, historic American visit, The Beatles came to Edinburgh. It was pandemonium. They sold 5,000 tickets for the shows they played at the old ABC cinema on Lothian Road. However, if you believed every Edinburgh person that says they went, you'd be looking at ten times that number. I am not one of those who will claim to have been there but I did see the huge fan reaction. The cinema was only a short walk up the road from where we stayed. Queues of girls and boys snaked from the cinema down the road and around the corner as far as the eye could see. Teenagers (them again) were camping outside the night before in their hundreds, hoping for entry. Police were buzzing everywhere, keeping order. The newspapers were full of it before, during and after. Two local girls had raised a petition to get the boys to come as I don't think Edinburgh was on the original schedule. If I remember the two girls that had kicked off the campaign didn't get into the show after all. It was a febrile, mad few days in my home town.

When it had all calmed down a bit, it got me thinking: those old *Jailhouse Rock* butterflies were dancing in my stomach again. I could form a group. I wouldn't have to front it or at least I could share the glare of attention and fame that would surely come my way. Why didn't I think of it before? It's obvious. It's my destiny. Where's Derek?

2

My Teenage Heart

I WAS BORN on 20 June 1948 in the Simpson Memorial Maternity Pavilion in Edinburgh, not too far from the family home at Smithfield Street, which was close to the Heart of Midlothian football stadium. The hospital was new when I came along and delivered around a third of million babies before it closed a few years ago to make way for posh flats for the burgeoning Edinburgh gentry. Local people knew it then, and fondly remember it now, as the Simpson's. I'm sure many notable people opened their eyes for the first time there but there are two individuals, especially, who I must mention.

The first was Stuart Sutcliffe, born three days after me but eight years earlier. He was an early member of The Beatles, having moved from Scotland to Liverpool as a boy and befriending John Lennon at art school. He died of a brain haemorrhage before the band broke through but because of that his mystique remains intact. Had he of lived would he have played at the ABC in April 1964? The other Simpson's baby, born seven years after me, was one Leslie Richard McKeown. More of him later.

We moved to Caledonian Road off the Dalry Road in an area sandwiched between Haymarket and Gorgie not long after my birth. It was a good working-class area, but I wouldn't say or never thought of it or us as deprived in any way. Our house was what was known as a 'colony house' – an identifying and loved feature of the Edinburgh outskirts, our ones being built in the mid-19th century to initially house employees of the Caledonian Railway. We had the ground floor flat which consisted of a large front room, two bedrooms, a box room, a kitchen and an indoor toilet.

Everyone congregated in the kitchen area, which had a double bed recess where our parents slept. Another feature was the big range, which was always fired up as Mum cooked one meal or another. Dad prepared only supper, the last meal before bed. Our bedrooms were warmed with paraffin heaters and in the winter, Mum ensured we all had hot water bottles for extra warmth. Both Mum and Dad smoked like chimneys. The house may have smelt of tobacco, but we wouldn't have noticed because all houses had that same Woodbine odour. Dad smoked Woodbines, he called them

Willie Woodbines, and Mum smoked Players. All the grown-ups smoked in the 1950s and 1960s. Indeed, the odd person that didn't puff was regarded with mild distrust. Then, being a non-smoker was almost as weird as being a vegetarian.

We had no bath or bathroom and to have a proper wash we used the Dalry Public Baths in Caledonian Crescent, almost next to us. I remember the Baths had a Brylcreem dispensing machine at a penny a squirt. Our old colony houses are much sought after now by professional people wanting easy access to the city.

Years later, when Derek and I were famous and globe-trotting, we'd be sure to bring home exotic drinks for a kind neighbour who lived upstairs from us who was the first in the tenement to install a bath. She'd allow us to use it rather than nip down to Dalry Baths. There was a time when two Bay City Rollers walking down Caledonian Road with their trunks rolled up in their towels heading for the Baths would have required a police cordon with army back-up.

My father, born in 1917, had the proud name of Duncan McIntosh Longmuir. His birthplace is recorded as HMP Perth. This does not indicate that he was a very juvenile delinquent; but that his Dad, my grandfather James Longmuir, was a Head Warden at the prison and here he met my grandmother, Janet Tait Laing, who was a prison warder.

My great-grandfather was also James Longmuir and he may have been born in Ireland. Around 1870 he married my great grandmother, Christina McIntosh from Inverness, and that is where my Dad got his middle name. James was a farmer and Christina a domestic servant. My mother was a child of Alexander Sim and Jane Birnie. He was a railway foreman from Kincardine and she hailed from Lairg, Sutherland. Our great-granddad on Mum's side, William Sim, is listed on the census as a teacher. So, perhaps, that is where I got my brains from (joke).

Dad had served in the Second World War with the Royal Engineers and seen action in several countries. He was in the Catering Corp owing to having been a butcher on civvy street before the war. On his return he firstly became a railway linesman and then landed a better position at St Cuthbert's Co-op as an undertaker, eventually becoming foreman. It was a decent job and I'm sure he was reasonably paid – he must have been because he was able to take a loan from his employer and eventually buy our flat. I may be mistaken but I think he paid £600 for it. He loved his job and carried himself as an undertaker should. In those days the funeral industry commanded respect like a doctor or teacher, although the qualifications needed were not as rigorous. Often, he would walk home in his full funeral service attire and people that didn't know him would remove their headwear or lower their heads and clasp their hands behind their backs in respect as he passed. On other occasions he would drop us children to school in the hearse or the firm ambulance with a very silent and cold passenger in a box in the back. Us kids loved it, thinking it was the height of irreverence from our old man.

At some point he met my mum, Georgina Alice Burnie Sim, a local girl who worked at the McVities biscuit factory. They were married in 1944, during the war, and Dad was in full uniform. My uncle Arthur was best man. We were a very happy family. Derek followed me into the world in 1951 and then, a few years later, my sisters Betty and Alice were born. I can picture Dad now, sitting in his chair in his creased trousers and vest with a straight back listening to the radio. My father was a little strict but never hit us. One look was enough to make us cease and desist whatever it was we were doing wrong. Unfortunately, Mum got landed disciplinary duties and sometimes she delivered a swift back-hander as Derek and I fought like cats and dogs over who got to listen to Radio Luxembourg. She was a good mum and a lovely lady. I'd give anything for a backhander from her now. I am pleased to report that the old flat, which holds so many memories for all of us siblings, remains in the family to this day.

Derek was into pop music from a very early age. I remember him buying *I'm A Boy* by The Who and *Dedicated to the One I Love* by the Mamas and Papas. On a Sunday he'd set up the Grundig reel to reel tape recorder to record *Pick of the Pops*, the Top 20 show hosted by Alan Freeman. Woe betide anyone who struck up a conversation or boiled a kettle while young Mastermix was on the job.

Before the television arrived (Dad got it on the knock from the Co-op) in the late 1950s or early 1960s, we played out in the streets. Football in the road had to be only occasionally interrupted by an approaching car. We'd pick up the ball, put it under our arm and wave to the driver. Normally he would wave back. I was okay at football and followed it a bit but was never fanatical. On a Saturday me and my cousin Neil would occasionally chance our arms and try to bunk into Tynecastle, home of Heart of Midlothian, by slipping under the big metal gates. The mighty Hearts. The team were winning everything in sight and I particularly recall a forward called Willie Bauld who the crowd idolised. When he got the ball the ground literally buzzed in anticipation. There was also a tough, young defender named Dave Mackay who would soon write his name large in the history of Scottish and English football.

Signs of the war were still around us. Some of the crescents and roads had gaps where houses and buildings once stood, like smiles missing a tooth. The adults spoke as if their lives had been cleaved in half. Everything was 'before the war' or 'since the war'. Dalry was a nice place to live. Everything we needed was around us. Out on the Dalry Road there was a wide array of shops selling just about everything. An early memory I have is the rag and bone man. He'd jolt into the road on his old horse and cart and ask for any old iron and any old anything else. A youth leant out a tenement window high up and said here you are mate and flicked down a coin. The rag and bone man leant down to pick it up and jumped up suddenly flinging the penny in the air and yelping like a dog.

'You young bastard,' he screamed waving his fist at an empty window. My neighbour had heated up a penny on the gas and thrown it down. Strange how some people passed the time.

Although I was happy in Dalry and its environs, I soon developed an affinity with the countryside. This all stemmed from regular visits to my granny's house a few miles outside of the City in a village called Lasswade. She owned a house with ten rooms and only now do I wonder how she got to afford that. We went there for our holidays and whenever else we could. My cousin, Neil Porteous, and I explored the fields, the banks of the River Esk and discovered nature. My love of animals, especially horses, was awakened here too. My Auntie Betty moved in with my granny and in many ways Lasswade was our second home. Neil was my relative, my friend, my classmate and, eventually, my band mate. He was a lovely pal to have.

As I said before, Dalry was not particularly rough or dangerous, but you did have to have your wits about you and be streetwise. I was never a fighter, but I can remember two incidents. One was with a boy who had been bullying Derek and I went and found him and gave him a wee bit of a hiding. I think that must have lulled me into a false sense of my pugilistic ability because at Tynecastle School I somehow got into a row with another laddie and this time he knocked seven bells out of me. Cousin Neil told me after that the boy was a British junior boxing champion. He could have told me before.

I got the work ethic very young. I did a paper round and a milk round. The milk round was with the Co-op (who else?) and I loved it. I worked with an old shire horse called Teddy who arguably was my first love. (Teddy gives me a tenuous connection to James Bond, by the way. Sean Connery was a milkman at the Co-op a decade or so before me and had worked with Teddy. He was Tommy or Tam Connery then and my Dad knew him well. Dad would often borrow him to clean out and polish the coffins.)

My first girlfriend was Sandra Stewart. She was a lovely, pretty girl who lived close by. I remember she had a friend called Penny and we'd all go to the youth club or the ice rink and she'd watch us rehearse in the front room at Caledonian Road. One day as we walked to the chip shop around the corner in Dalry Road she told me her family were moving to Glasgow – she would still be in Scotland but in those days it might as well have been Australia. I never saw her again and always had the hope that one day she'd make contact. After I became famous I had a few letters and approaches from past female acquaintances, but Sandra wasn't one of them. I expect she married someone with a proper job.

Generally, I was very happy at my schools – Dalry Primary and Tyne-castle Secondary. I wasn't a great pupil but I wasn't a bad one either. There was a metalwork teacher I feared called Mr Pearson. He was prone to quick bursts of temper and occasionally I was on the end of a whack from him. However, there was an altogether more sinister master named Mr Gray and he patrolled the classroom with a forked leather belt draped theatrically over his shoulder. If you committed the sin of talking he'd pounce and make you stand up and then deliver a double-hander with the belt. Looking back now I realise how strange his behaviour was, bordering on sadism, I'd say. I got a few blows from him, but I never thought of telling my Dad. In those day parents and teachers stuck solidly by each other and my guess was Dad would have taken the line that if the master believed I deserved the belt then I deserved the belt. Also, I was not unusual to be on the receiving end of what they called corporal punishment (more palatable than 'beating little children with leather straps') – it was all part of the package.

Dad may have been more alarmed had I told him about another teacher we had called Percy. This bloke was the opposite of violent and used to take us for swimming lessons weekly. He was famous among us boys for being very keen on demonstrating the importance of the buoyancy of buttocks when swimming. We thought it was a great giggle splashing away from him as soon as we had immersed ourselves in the great rush not to be his guinea pig for the morning. I would be surprised if any of my teachers, and few of my peers, would remember me long after 1963 when I left armed with my Edinburgh School Certificate to join the world of employment.

I remember that summer well. I was gagging to get out to work and put money in my pocket, wanting to play with the big boys, even though I was only 14 or 15. It was all going on. The Beatles were number one with *From Me to You* and building up a head of steam. *Dr No*, featuring suave secret agent James Bond, was the must-see film (though we couldn't take it too seriously as it starred our old milkman) and the talk in every pub and front room was of a bunch of crooks robbing the Glasgow train of millions of pounds. I cannot recall anybody being critical of the thieves. It was like Jesse James and Robin Hood had joined forces to relieve the Sheriff of Nottingham of his ill-gotten gains.

Harold MacMillan was our Prime Minister. He claimed to be Scottish, but we had our doubts. The old guy just seemed to personify the much talked about 'generation gap'. He looked about 90 and mumbled and moved like he was senile when he retired on the grounds of ill-health. Now I know he was only a mere 69 years old! Younger than I am now. While he was wrestling with the fall-out from the Profumo scandal and we hanged our last convicted murderer here in Scotland, a little TV show had started being broadcast that would stir the kids up even more and was a big influence on me.

Ready Steady Go! was fantastic. Shown on a Friday evening, it was a live music show heralded with the strap line 'The Weekend Starts Here'. Yes, it did. It tapped into the emerging Mod scene and had an urgency and impromptu feel. We were Mods in the mid-sixties, buying our sharp, made-to-measure suits from Burtons on the North Bridge. On *RSG!*, cameras swung around capturing cool looking teenagers in the best polo-necks stylishly dancing to the latest acts. I first heard Tamla Motown, The Supremes, Marvin Gaye, Big Dee Irwin and The Temptations on that show. Up until then the only black artists we'd come across were Nat King Cole and Sammy Davis Jnr. We had The Beatles unlocking our emerging personalities and the black acts unlocking our souls.

I must have been so taken with Tamla Motown that for a short while we called the developing band The Motown Stompers. I had forgotten this – it must have been for a very short time – but my old Edinburgh contemporary and friend from The Hipple People, Dave Valentine, coincidentally turned up at my local pub recently when he had been fishing nearby and assured me this was the case.

Then The Who appeared and their performance knocked me out. I later was able to see them live. I remember standing mesmerised at the front, looking up at Pete Townsend attacking his guitar. Their drummer, Keith Moon, grimaced as he pounded like a madman. He really was a madman and one day I'd witness him in full flow. Us youngsters could not wait to finish work on a Friday, absorb *Ready Steady Go!* and get out on the town, to the pub in the first years and then later the night spots of Edinburgh.

When I left school, Dad, got me an interview with the Co-op as an invoice clerk in a large office. I took a brief exam and I was in. I hated it from day one. I felt like an extra in a Norman Wisdom film. We sat one to a desk in rows, wearing almost identical suits and ties with our paper clips and fingerettes organised regimentally in front of us. Our task was to add up invoice totals. No calculators. Nothing else. No talking. No interaction. For me it was hell on earth. I was there nine months and the only good thing is it may have helped me keep track of the Bay City Rollers money had we ever had seen any of it. Our office was opposite Edinburgh Palais and I didn't know it then but there was a guy leading the big band over there called Tam Paton. We hadn't met yet, but we were to change each other's lives dramatically within a decade.

The money at the Co-op wasn't bad at £4 a week but it was soul zapping and I needed to get out. They gave us Wednesdays off and I would use that time searching for another job. I finally landed one at Kyles & Son, based at The Haymarket, not far around the corner from where we stayed in Caledonian Road. Kyles was a builders ran by two brothers and they offered me an apprenticeship as a plumber. My apprenticeship certificate, which I have to this day, shows I signed on the dotted line on 6 April 1964. The money was less at three quid every week and I paid my Mum ten shillings a week keep, but I had my eye on the future and a career I might enjoy. I should have paid Mum more, but we came to an agreement that I would buy my own clothes as 'gear' was becoming more important by the day. Most of my wages went on the latest and ever-changing Mod fashions although invariably were purchased with Provident cheques. These were effectively small personal loans repaid at an agreed rate via the Provy Man who would turn up at the door like a bad penny once a week for his pound of flesh.

At Kyles they called me 'Boy' and it was abundantly clear I was bottom of the pile, but it was one of the best moves I ever made. Being cooped up in an office was not for me. The plumbing trade entailed a degree of independence, meeting the public and the promise of something different every day. Plumbing was to keep my head above water (or worse) several times in my life. Even then I was still doing my paper round before I started work in the morning to get extra cash. I didn't resent this at all as I needed the money for buying the latest clothes from Burton's and the like. On a Saturday I had to deliver the *Pink News* and they had a double edition to cater for the football results. I resented that because I was itching to get out. Saturday night was the night.

I knew I was becoming a man when after work I could go for a bevy with my workmates in Ryrie's pub across the road from the yard and down at the other end of the bar was my old man, often in his funeral attire. We didn't speak until we got indoors, both respecting each other's privacies. I wouldn't stay in the pub long as I wanted to get home, have some scran and get rehearsing because, by now, we had the band up and running. We even had a name: The Saxons.

Edinburgh had an incredible club and music scene in the 1960s and, although I was a huge fan of The Beatles, The Stones, The Hollies and Manfred Mann, there was a feast of local bands who I admired just as much. Disco hadn't quite been invented, therefore all the clubs had live bands to pull the crowds in and it was very competitive. I would watch them all and observed their bass guitarists like a hawk, seeing how they played their chords, noting how they handled their guitars. I particularly remember The Beachcombers, The Embers, The Hipple People, The Moonrakers, Three's-A-Crowd, The Hunters, Tony and the Traders and The Crusaders. The Beachcombers, I believe, went down to London and cut a record but it didn't chart; The Hipple People had an enthusiastic following; but The Crusaders were considered by many to be Edinburgh's best group and the ones most likely to hit the big time.

Tam Paton had managed and played keyboard for The Crusaders, as well as managing The Hipple People, before he set up his big band at the Palais and supported national bands on tours of the UK. He claimed to have supported The Beatles, but I expect he made this up as he was never very specific on the details. The story Tam often told, which I do believe to be accurate, was that he had been playing keyboards with the Crusaders when the band went down to London to compete in the National Beat Group Competition at the Prince of Wales Theatre. The judges included Cilla Black, Ringo Starr, Alan 'Fluff' Freeman and The Beatles' manager Brian Epstein. It must have been very early in The Beatles' career for Ringo to be judging a talent show as, by 1966, he'd have been beyond all that. A Beatle couldn't settle his paper bill without a riot. The Crusaders didn't win but Tam thought they should have and took Brian Epstein to task demanding to know why they didn't get the votes (Will Young did a similar thing to Simon Cowell a few decades later). Epstein explained that the judges felt the boys were a good enough 'show band' but lacked originality, spark and, most importantly, image. When Tam moved on from his big band into pop management fully he would heed Epstein's advice. For Paton, 'image' was to trump everything else.

Meanwhile, back in the front room at 5 Caledonian Road, we were practising like mad. Derek had got a set of Ringo Starr drums soon to be replaced by an even better kit and I had a Rosetti electric guitar. It was my pride and joy. I'd got a ScotLoan from the Bank of Scotland to pay for it and some amplifiers. I was in hock to the tune of £7 a month – big debt at the time. I was determined to play better and, besides watching the bass players in the Edinburgh bands and studying the obligatory Bert Weedon's *Play in a Day* manual, I got lessons from a guy called Scott Murray. Scott loved music, had a music shop and could play guitar well. He patiently taught me new chords and techniques, taking me beyond Buddy Holly three-chord riffs. He loved watching the band develop and was a real help and support in our formative days. He even agreed to drive us to gigs in our hired van. I remember once playing a very early booking in Romanno Bridge in Peeblesshire and Scott drove. We were being paid £10 but it cost £12 to hire the van and that's before putting the petrol in. We owe Scott a great deal.

Derek, Neil and I began to feel a little like a pop group, our confidence growing daily but we knew we needed to move it on, so we began to think about how to progress. To be honest none of us were natural front men so when Derek bought home his new pal from Tynecastle School as a potential member of the band we knew immediately that we had found our lead singer. Gordon Clark was only 15 or 16 but he was good-looking, had no qualms about getting up and singing and we liked him. He was nicknamed Nobby, but not by us. It was then, and possibly still is, compulsory to call anyone with the surname Clark, Nobby; although Petula and Dave seem to have been exceptions to this rule.

Around this point I put a small advert in the *Evening News* for another new band member. We had some cranks present themselves for auditions at the house and can remember Derek and I trying not to look at one another to avoid giggling as we tried to bring totally unsuitable candidates to a quick conclusion without hurting their feelings. Then a 16-year-old laddie named Dave Pettigrew arrived with his guitar and impressed us. He was quiet and smartly dressed hailing from the well-to-do Oxgangs area of Edinburgh. He handled his instrument like a pro and knew all The Beatles numbers, even the ones that were harder to play. We gave him the job there and then. Dave made us a better unit there was no doubt. Our repertoire widened, and we were louder and tighter. He was a quiet boy who didn't say too much so naturally we nicknamed him Dave the Rave.

Now we thought we were a 'proper' pop group. It was 1965 – a lively time. Mods and Rockers were terrorising seaside resorts not even paying the 2d for the deckchairs they were lobbing at one another. The Beatles and The Rolling Stones were still dominant but The Kinks, The Hollies, The Animals, Herman's Hermits and the exciting bands from America like The Four Tops, The Supremes and The Temptations were all important parts of the musical landscape. There must have been stuff going on in the wider world, but we didn't know or care. We knew, for example, something was happening in Vietnam, but paid scant attention. It was The Saxons, the music, the scene. Nothing else mattered. We rehearsed most days. Mum and Dad were very patient indulging us, probably hoping we'd grow out of it soon. The music emanating from the house was even attracting girls who were drawn to the beat and hung around outside giggling as we went in and out. We thought we were in touching distance of being pop stars, but we'd never played on a stage in front of an audience.

Roller history has it that our first ever gig was at the Cairns Church youth club. It was certainly our first paid appearance, but Derek recently reminded me that the three of us –Derek, Neil and I – auditioned for something or other at the Ross Bandstand in Princes' Street Gardens. I remember it now, but I would be surprised if anybody else does. If they were there they witnessed the very first public incarnation of the group that would become the Bay City Rollers as early as 1965. Derek thinks we played a Kinks number. I can't remember and, whatever we were auditioning for, we didn't qualify.

Later when the five of us were in place we made our professional debut. That would be me, Derek, Neil, Nobby and Dave the Rave. I say professional only in the sense that we were hired and paid. The Cairns Church youth club down on Gorgie Road had a band booked to play on a Saturday night and they pulled out at the last minute. Someone suggested we could stand in. Probably one of the giggling girls from outside the house. We said yes. I don't remember what money they offered us. They probably gave us a free hymn book each. I do remember I was scared. It was all well and good bashing away in our own front room playing to a less than critical mother and father and baby sisters, but this was on a stage in front of people. Real people.

I don't remember what we opened with but there was a few Beatles numbers in there. You couldn't go wrong with the Fab Four in 1965. Nobby was great. He had the job of remembering all the words. It was alright for us we just had to remember the harmonies and the chords. In most of these cases – Yeah, Yeah, Yeah. All credit to him. He had a record player indoors and would buy the new singles and play them over and over until he had the words off pat. No mean feat. We also had some crib sheets taped secretly here and there as prompts. Nobby just stood there at first but soon realised him moving caused a reaction. He was a natural and just got better. There was no screaming, but the girls pushed to the front and looked up adoringly finding it hard to keep still. Many of them were from or had been to Tyne-castle School with us and Derek and Nobby especially, which helped. They wanted to like us. However, I noticed some of the boys were not so keen. Standing with their backs to the walls looking a bit hostile. It was a tiny hint of what lay in store.

The youth club gig had given us confidence and we knew, to move forward, we had to get bookings and perform at venues where we didn't have the benefit of such a sympathetic audience. I decided that each one of us would go into town and hustle at the pubs and clubs to book the band. None of us were over eighteen and of the legal drinking age although I was more or less there and had been frequenting these places for a couple of years. What some of these venue owners thought though when Derek, for instance, turned up trying to persuade them to book his band, I don't know. I just hoped his pencil sharpener and sling didn't fall out his pocket.

Unbelievably, we got some gigs. Early slots supporting others mainly, but we were soon on stage regularly learning our craft. All the bad things happened. Sometimes Nobby forgot his words. Sometimes I came in playing the wrong number. Sometimes we'd stop a song and start again. Occasionally one of us would stumble and fall. It was our apprenticeship not much different from plumbing where I had to learn all the tools and what they did. Pick up the tricks of the trade as I went. Often, in those first days, we'd play to an indifferent audience. Sometimes we'd play to *no* audience. But, because expectation was not high, and we were often time-filling we were allowed space and time to hone our act and we *were* getting better all the time.

I went to college once a week as part of my plumbing apprenticeship and here I met Greig Ellison who was also studying. I soon learned he played guitar. It was amazing how many people were playing an instrument and/or in a band at that time. It is testament to the hold pop music had on the nation's youth in the mid-sixties. I got Greig back to the Edinburgh School of Modern Music (the front room at Caledonian Road) and he knocked us out with his guitar-playing ability. He was great. He was in.

It was 1966, I believe a small colony of Scotland had just won a piddly football tournament called the World Cup.

Soon after, Greig's brother, Mike, joined the band. He too was a nice guy and became our second singer. I guess by having two vocalists we were trying to emulate The Hipple People who were, in 1967, Edinburgh's top band. Ian Nichol and Dave Valentine fronted them, and they were everywhere playing all the clubs I frequented like The Gonk, McGoos, The International and The Top Storey Club. The Hipple People were different, accomplished and had an adventurous set including lesser known songs like the Stones track *Time Is On My Side* and Marvin Gaye's *I'll Be Doggone*. They were managed by Tam Paton whose name kept coming up. It didn't last too long with Mike, perhaps Nobby didn't welcome the competition. Perhaps, we were confusing the fans by having too many line-up changes as we were building up a following by now. Mike left and we were five again.

Here we were playing mainly local gigs, we were a tight outfit with a bit of a following but I knew exactly what we needed. Not another band member. No. We needed a manager. And I knew exactly who.

3
Dedication

TAM PATON WAS a face in Edinburgh. I was familiar with him not only as a member of The Crusaders but currently as the leader of his big band in the Palais de Danse. We called him the one-armed pianist as he waved when we came in (as he did to everyone) but the piano kept playing with his other arm. He was centre-stage on a revolving stage – an idea they may have nicked from TV's *Sunday Night at the London Palladium*, or more likely the other way around. Tam revolving, waving with a rictus smile on his face is a memory I will always hold. Beneath the revolving stage was a couple of guys hand cranking its motion. We found this hilarious, joking that, when at home, they walked in circles around their front rooms spinning their hands in a circular fashion while their wives tried to get them to sit down. There was a touch of Monty Python about the set-up. Who knows if Tam was wearing trousers behind the cover of his piano?

The Palais, now demolished after spending its old age masquerading as a bingo hall, evokes special memories for many of the older folk who stayed in Edinburgh. It was a grand, white fronted, art-deco building that had been built at the turn of the 20th century. It has been a skating rink and a cinema, but, for all my young life, it was a dance hall, *the* dance hall. If civil laws required Edinburgh couples to declare where they met on their marriage certificates the Palais name would crop up comfortably ten more times than any other place. Some nights, when it was rocking, nearly a thousand people glided around the dance floor. Although, it was a couple's place and, unbelievably, did not serve alcohol, there was sometimes vicious fights. Legend has it that Sean Connery, who was a bouncer at the Palais for a while, single-handedly bashed up a few members of the notorious Valdor gang whose reputation permeated Edinburgh street mythology. Fights persisted after Connery's time and it was rumoured that Tam Paton was not averse to jumping off the rostrum and getting stuck in. Tam was known as a tough guy in Edinburgh. He wouldn't take shit from anyone. He was also part of the last generation to do national service although, strangely, he rarely mentioned it.

He was a solid, stocky man with noticeably broad shoulders. His dark hair, brushed over at the side to disguise early thinning of his thatch, reminds me now of the singer Neil Diamond in middle age. He was charismatic and had an aura about him. Being ten years older than me and an established figure on the music scene, I was certainly in awe of him. The broad shoulders were honed through years of carrying sacks of potatoes – his daytime job in his successful family business run by his parents from their home in the Prestonpans area east of Edinburgh. Later, when familiarity *had* bred contempt, we nicknamed him Tatty Tam because of this and The Late Tam Paton due to his infuriating habit of being tardy for everything.

Before I ever asked him to manage us, he had already moved us on as a band with a throwaway remark: when we were out touting around the clubs in town for gigs, Greig Ellison and I ventured in to The Top Storey Club, above Burtons on Leith Street. The club was run by two brothers called Craig – another pair of Edinburgh men you wouldn't want to cross. We approached Jimmy Craig who was in deep conversation with none other than Tam Paton, apologised for interrupting, introduced ourselves as The Saxons and asked if there was any chance of any work.

Jimmy threw it over to Tam: 'Are they any guid?'

'Aye, they're guid,' says Tam and Jimmy booked us.

To this day I will never know whether this was a wonderful act of munificence on Tam's part or whether he didn't want to admit to Jimmy that he didn't know everything about the Edinburgh music scene. Whatever the reason, it was a defining moment because we were given the regular Saturday night slot at The Top Storey on Tam's say. This built our reputation and we started to build a strong, loyal and vociferous female following. The Top Storey got us noticed and, in time, people were coming to see us, not the outfits we were supporting. Those outfits included Tam's protégés The Hipple People and The Beachcombers.

I saw Herman's Hermits at The Top Storey and they impressed me no end. Peter Noone, the lead singer, was older than me but looked about 13. He and his band were a consummate act from Manchester and the crowd loved them, yet in the music press they were not taken very seriously and a lot of their material was dismissed as 'commercial'. I never understood, and still don't, why 'commercial' was a bad thing. I thought that was the general idea. America, however, welcomed them with open arms. They even made a film in the States called *Hold Tight!* It went down well, although over here not so much. When one critic compared it to The Beatles film *Help!* another reviewer said the only similarity was the exclamation mark. I would learn more about these lofty and parochial attitudes in time.

Another class band I recall from The Top Storey was The Warriors, also from England. Their lead singer was Jon Anderson who, like us, would have to wait for the next decade to enjoy success, in his case with the progressive rock band Yes. Local band The Jury went psychedelic and changed their name to The Writing on the Wall. There was a buzz about them for a while and they went down to London where John Peel championed them. Sadly, the writing was on the wall for them when they had all their gear pinched in the Big Smoke and they drifted apart.

Nobby's girlfriend at the time harangued me to ask Tam to manage us. Tam was the obvious man to go to, but I was scared of approaching him even though he had said 'Aye, they're guid'. Eventually I plucked up the courage and I waylaid him at the Palais. He muttered something about being busy and bearing us in mind. So, I then started to pester him on the telephone.

Sometime in 1967 Tam Paton finally agreed to come to the house and watch us play. Many accounts have him turning up with the Radio Luxembourg disc-jockey Glaswegian Stuart Henry, but that was not the case. Stuart was a great friend to the group even after he progressed from Radio Scotland, a pirate station, to the newly-launched BBC Radio 1. He was an amiable, funny and generous soul who for some reason took a shine to the Rollers and found us engagements and generally championed us. But it was not Stuart that rocked up with Tam that day, instead it was Kenny Maclean, manager of The Beachcombers and whose son played drums in the band.

We were all keyed up, anxious to impress. Having Tam turn up at the house in a flash car was a big deal. He was a local celebrity. Every chip shop owner in Edinburgh knew him – he delivered their spuds. We knew a great deal depended on this meeting. Mum and Dad were hovering in the background, our apprehension feeding into them. I'm told we played *Please Mr Postman*, a song that was co-written by Brian Holland, later of the song-writing partnership Holland-Dozier-Holland, and was the first Tamla Motown number, when recorded by The Marvelettes, to make number one in the US Billboard charts. It was made even more popular over here when The Beatles recorded it as a track on their *With The Beatles* LP. We rattled through that and a couple of others. I don't think we performed well. We were pent up and stiff. Tam thanked us and said he'd be in touch. In most languages that means thanks, but no thanks.

He later told me that he had said in the car to Kenny, 'What do you reckon?'.

'They'll do nothing,' was Kenny's reply.

Tam said it was then he decided he would manage us. He would have taken Maclean's dismissal as a competitive challenge as they were rivals. So, his agreement to take us on was based on as much as a 'I'll show you' kneejerk reaction as any spark of talent and promise he saw in us. I believe this really was the case. I can remember Tam, recalling the moment in his later years (after rivers of bad blood had flowed between us all), saying that he too thought we were not much cop but were pretty young things that he could mould into something and build an image around. Tam was expert in rewriting history, as we will see.

As we became more serious and focussed, Neil Porteous had different priorities. And who could blame him? He was head-over-heels in love with his school sweetheart, a really smashing girl called Fiona. Neil began to miss rehearsals and then he was gone. No dramas. No bad feelings. He'd moved on. I am pleased to say he married Fiona. I don't believe he had any regrets about missing out on what came next. Who knows? Perhaps he saw what was coming? I think easing Neil out could have been one of Tam's first moves. He saw Neil was in love and that it wasn't with him. Tam demanded total dedication to the band, to the cause, to him. Neil was not rebellious at all, but Tam could not bear playing second fiddle to a woman. Whatever. Then we were four.

Paton's impact was immediate. He got us gigs across Scotland and beyond. For the first time, we performed in England and, in time, the northern club circuit became a mainstay of our schedule. Tam did a deal with the London agency Starlight who dubbed it the 'chicken-in-a-basket' circuit. At first it was a refreshing change from the chaos and underlying violence of the Scottish dance hall scene. Chicken sandwiches were the order of the day as opposed to knuckle sandwiches. We would find ourselves back on Starlight's rota more than once in our careers.

If any readers can recall a bizarre TV programme from the 1970s called *The Wheeltappers and Shunters Social Club,* that describes our experience in those early days pretty much spot on. Here we were playing to a different crowd. Or, should I say, an indifferent one. There was no loyal and appreciative fan base like the one we now had in Edinburgh. This audience were older, more male and focused on enjoying their light and mild, not us. They livened up a bit for the comedian, but the music was merely a backdrop. It paid though.

One night we were halfway through *Mrs Robinson* and the compère – an outgrown Teddy Boy with a greased-back quiff – waddled on in front of us. He waved us to 'simmer down' and took the microphone from Nobby's hands.

'Ladies and Gentlemen,' he said. 'Just to let you know steak and kidney pies and chips now being served at the long bar. Hurry yourselves up before the gannets at the back sink 'em all. Bingo's at nine when this lot have finished.' He handed the mike back to Nobby and nodded at us to resume. We were gobsmacked.

Another time we were in some other northern English mining town and were at the side of stage killing time before we were due on after the next act. The compère, a different man, of course, but who looked very similar to the previous one – like Ted Bovis in *Hi Di Hi* – cleared his throat and began:

'Ladies and Gents. Next on we have an act all the way from America. Yes, America. They're a couple of darkies called Mac and Katie Kissoon. Not my cup of tea. But you might like 'em.'

Derek and I visibly winced and exchanged horrified looks. Things were different then, but this was awful. I don't even think the old fool was trying to be funny.

Once we played a miner's club in Whitburn. We had just won a thing called 'Most Professional Group in Edinburgh' and were feeling quite pleased with our ascendancy. Again, there was a compère present and we were lurking behind the big curtain chatting to the guy. Whilst we were there, I realised that the audience was unnaturally silent. I stepped forward, parted the curtain to take a peep and to my horror we, the band, outnumbered the audience. Four people dotted the seats. I nudged Nobby.

'There's nobody out there.'

Nobby had a look. He turned to the compère.

'There's nobody out there.'

The compère gave him an old-fashioned look and swept one of the curtains aside prompting me and Nobby to jump back, embarrassed.

'Yes, there is,' he chided. 'Now, let me get it right, so you're the Beige City Rollers and you've just won the most progressive group in Edinburgh…'

I looked him at him in despair.

'You're not… you're not going to…'

'Introduce you? Course I am. That's my job.'

And he did. Bold as brass. And we played, the spotlights picking us out for further ridicule. It wasn't a gig it was an intrusion.

Mind you the money was coming in, at last. We had as much work as we could cope with. We were playing every Friday and Saturday and the odd gig during the week. We got a residency at the International Club on a Saturday.

The International had launched in 1965 with Glasgow Rangers football icon Jim Baxter doing the honours. We'd play an early set, rush off to The Top Storey, do a session there and then we'd go back to The International to close. By that time, it would be 3am and the adrenalin would be coursing through us. We'd go down to the Metropole Café on Torphichen Place in Haymarket, which was run by a charming old Italian couple. Here we'd meet a variety of artists all hanging out there having finished their gigs. The band vans would park up outside identifiable by fan graffiti. The musicians all mixed in here and we all got to know each other. I made friends with the enigmatic Linnie Paterson, the lead singer of The Jury. He had a charisma about him and everyone thought that if anybody was going to make it, he would. The first time I ever ate Spaghetti Bolognese was in there. I remember being star struck sitting at a table next to Marty Wilde and spotting Donald Peers across the room (look him up). Marty still performs in his 80s, so there's hope for me yet.

The good news was that we were getting paid as much as £40 a night. To put this in perspective, I was probably only earning £4 a week as a plumber's apprentice. We all had day jobs so we were starting to feel a bit flush. I was plumbing, Derek and Nobby were joiners. It was a slog, but we had high hopes because, with Tam spearheading our charge, we were convinced we were going to break into the big time. We had momentum.

Meanwhile we had decided to change our name. We had toyed with others, notably 'The Deadbeats' but knew that was going nowhere, but we also knew that 'The Saxons' was so early 1960s. I wanted something that evoked speed and the USA. 'Mitch Ryder and the Detroit Wheels' was a name that had captured my imagination. You cannot underestimate the deferential attitude most people had to American culture at the time – it was generally accepted then that we, in the UK, were 30 years behind them in most things. Their films were superior. Their clothes were smarter. As a society we aspired to be American. One of us had already thrown 'Rollers' into the mix and I decided we needed an American place name before it. Rollers evoked the sense of speed I was looking for and could also be interpreted to refer to rock and rollers. A map was produced one day at Tam's family premises in Prestonpans and I threw a dart at it. I'm not claiming the arrow landed dead on Bay City, Michigan but most of the place names close by were unsuitable. Bad Axe Rollers? I don't think so. Bay City Rollers rolled off the tongue. It had symmetry and we were all comfortable with it straight away.

Derek now tells me it was he who threw the dart. Who am I to argue? If he is going to claim credit for the dart-throwing, I will claim ownership of the dart itself. It was Tam's family map, so let us settle on a joint effort.

I'd like to say we put Bay City on the map. There are a few Bay Citys in America, however none of them have claimed us as their own. Bay City in Michigan, it seems, are cautious about pinning the town's colours to pop stars. Madonna, probably the most successful female recording artist of all time, was born there and from what I hear she is not really celebrated in Bay City. Whether this is connected to her saying in an interview once that 'Bay City was a smelly little town', I don't know.

As the first serious cash began to flow in, Tam invented the concept of the pot, but there was no physical pot. He said all the money went into the pot and from that pot all expenses would be paid and then, when and if the pot allowed, the surplus would be divided equally six ways – the five band members and Tam. This seemed a fair and democratic division of the fruits of our labour to us and Tam seemed happy for Derek, who was always careful with his paper round money, to keep tabs on all this, too. After gigs we'd go for a Chinese meal and Derek would settle the bill out of the pot (Tam liked going for meals following gigs. It kept us from drifting off to nightspots where we might meet loose women and imbibe alcohol). When the pot built a reasonable surplus, we'd invest it in assets. At one point we were running such a surplus that we put a deposit down and bought a brand spanking new Mercedes van. The other Edinburgh bands were green with envy. The pot seemed a good and democratic notion. I used to dream about the pot and when it would be emptied and divvied up. I still do.

4
Give It to Me Now

ALTHOUGH TAM WAS making a difference, we were just one of the many balls he had spinning in the air. He still had his orchestra, helped run the family potato wholesale business, managed other bands and was a promoter to boot. He wore this latter hat on the occasion that we supported The Bee Gees.

It was 1967 and, in a small place called Rosewell, about ten miles from the house, Tam had made a booking for The Bee Gees. This booking had been agreed before the boys had broken through to the big time so the band had to honour it. The Bee Gees had just had had two minor hits but with two very strong numbers, *New York Mining Disaster 1941* and *To Love Somebody.* However, by the time this concert had come around they were riding high at the top of the charts with *Massachusetts.* They were hot property. The place was bursting to the seams and the smile on Tam's face could have powered our amps. We watched from the side of the stage salivating over their gleaming and sophisticated equipment and marvelling at their ability. I knew they would become massive. The intuitive vocal power of the Gibb brothers was spellbinding, and Colin Peterson on drums and Vince Melouney on lead guitar completed a powerful unit. We exchanged a few words and wishes of good luck with them.

We played Rosewell another time supporting Band of Joy who featured Robert Plant and John Bonham, who not so long later would form Led Zeppelin. The next time we'd meet The Bee Gees, though, would be back on the treadmill of the club circuit in Sheffield Hallam in reduced circumstances for them. I guess it was 1974. We were in our ascendancy and they sat us down and gave us a fatherly talking to. The business is full of crooks, they warned. Don't sign anything, they urged. They're all sharks even the ones that seem trustworthy. They told us about bands we knew of who had had big hits but when they asked their managers and producers where the money had gone, they said it had been spent in production and promotion costs. The bands remonstrated and said it was unfair. Sue me! challenged the managers, knowing they did not have the financial resources to do so. The

Bee Gees themselves obviously had their fingers burned too, but we were pinching salt and throwing it over our shoulders as they spoke. But we had Tam, we thought. Tam was one of us. However, one day the Gibb brothers' words would ring very true for us and, although they had no idea, they were just a few years away themselves from conquering the world a second time and accumulating riches that they could only have dreamed of. How fickle is show business? You could write a book about it.

Barry Gibb ended up marrying a local girl, Linda Gray from Mussel-burgh and I was always under the impression they met at that Rosewell gig. Linda was Miss Edinburgh and I assumed they were introduced backstage; however Barry said in a TV interview recently that they met at the *Top of the Pops* studio and were introduced by Jimmy Savile.

I vaguely remember Savile being at Rosewell, but we met him several times so cannot be sure. One time he picked Nobby above his head and held him aloft in a wrestling pose. He had been a wrestler in his early days (Savile, not Nobby). It would be tempting here to claim that I always felt uncomfortable around and about him, but I didn't. I shared a long car jour-ney alone with him once and there was no salaciousness or any red flags at all. Not that I remember. He was an eccentric for sure and an unashamed self-publicist but if you compared him against other exhibitionist wrestlers of the period, Big Daddy, for example, he didn't set off any alarm bells. I regarded him as a far less talented Ken Dodd of tickling stick fame. Jimmy roped us into a couple of his charity walks which were early wheezes by Tam to get us into the papers. We posed for publicity shots at the beginning and maybe at the end. I'm pretty sure I, at least, didn't actually walk any 20-milers.

Savile was tactile – I do remember that – with males and females. But a lot of people were. It was a different age though. Sexual abuse had not yet been outed although time has shown how prevalent it actually was. It was a practice, we thought (if we ever thought about it at all) confined to men in macs. Flashers and pervs were figures of fun. When things are not in your comprehension you simply don't comprehend them.

We had now built a more modern sound-proofed rehearsal room-cum-studio at the back of Tam's parents' potato warehouse in Prestonpans. Much to my Mum and Dad's relief, 'Bay City Rollers Central' had relocated. A fan club of sorts was evolving, and our point of contact was Wilma. The fans imagined Wilma to be a young fan herself who had taken over the secretarial side of Rollers' activity. She was in fact Tam's mum. She and Tam's old man were a lovely couple who were hugely supportive of their entrepreneurial son. Tam's Dad would sit in his old armchair, taking in all the goings on, and would occasionally lean forward, sniff loudly and then emit a gob of spit into the hearth like a Barn Owl expelling a pellet. It wasn't pleasant, but you got used to it.

Meanwhile, Nobby showed a flair for making his own clothes. Up until now we'd been straitjacketed often in dress suits and bow ties, especially on the circuit. The clothes Nobby was adapting for himself, and then us, were starting to give us a more individual look. A style was emerging. Tam wasn't sure in which direction to take us, but he did know – because Brian Epstein's words were imprinted in his brain – that we had to have an image if we were going to capture the wider public's imagination. Tam was just waiting for an inspiration or gimmick.

Now and then I'd ask Tam how the pot was going. He explained that, as we grew, so did our costs. With the continuing investment we had to make in musical instruments, the significant expense of getting to and from gigs and now, more frequently, the overnight stays in the different gig locations, we had yet to receive any money of our own. This seemed logical and pragmatic – Derek thought so too. Tam then went on to suggest that we all took a weekly wage as part of the expenses before any carve-up of profits. This was a welcome idea and I was sufficiently encouraged to pack up plumbing at the end of 1970 and become a professional musician.

Derek took the plunge at the same time. He hadn't enjoyed school at all. The only teacher he had any connection with was his woodwork master and because of that he had pursued a career as a joiner when he was just 14. He ended up working for a big construction firm, James Miller, who are still around today as Miller Homes. When he told them he was leaving to pursue a career with the band his foreman, Neal, sat him down and said:

'Derek, get a grip. It's a crazy dream. You're not thinking straight. You really need to think this thing through.'

'I have thought it through,' said Derek. 'We're going to be massive.'

Neal shook his head. Impetuous kids.

There was no going back now. I was fully committed. I don't think any of the band were in it for just money, though. We were young, and we didn't dream of riches. We dreamt of fame and the adulation of females and the admiration of males. We wanted the rock 'n' roll lifestyle, of lying on sun-loungers in Beverly Hills, of hobnobbing with The Beatles in London's Bag O Nails night spot, of locking ourselves in a studio and producing landmark albums. Money would be a nice and handy by-product of all of this.

The period between 1967 and 1970 saw several line-up changes, none of which upset the balance of the band too much. It has been presented, sometimes by Tam himself, that the member changes were part of a ruthless strategy to create the perfect band. Or should I say the perfect brand? Tam didn't even survive into the Simon Cowell era but that's how he saw himself when he viewed the whole story through the prism of hindsight. The great puppet master. The grand architect. He who controls all. But it really was not like that. Most people who left did so because they wanted to, Tam and the rest of us had to react and adapt to keep the show on the road.

When Mike Ellison left it may have been Tam's idea, but I don't think Mike was too bothered. The two singers thing was a gimmick. Others, like Mike's brother, Greig, also left eventually. The main reason they departed was Tam's controlling nature and the sheer arduousness of the job. Three years is a long time when you are trying to be famous, driving around the country inhaling each other's farts and belches in clapped out Ford Transits, singing the same covers and only having covert intimate contact with the opposite sex, which was positively unhealthy.

As soon as Tam witnessed the female adulation we were receiving in Edinburgh he made a policy decision. He told us that were not to have girl-friends. It was implicit that if one of us decided to marry we'd be an ex-Bay City Roller. He said that if it was discovered one of us had a girlfriend it would ruin the illusion and the female following would fall away and we'd be finished as a band. He cited the case of John and Cynthia Lennon and told us how Brian Epstein was forced to keep their marriage a secret and, when it did come out, all hell was let loose. Personally, I didn't think John Lennon had too bad a career after he was married, but wasn't going to say that to Tam. I could see the logic of what he was saying and, such was our devotion to and faith in him, we went along with it. More or less. I, for one, did have female attachments and Tam either never found out or wasn't too bothered about me, perhaps because I was older. But, Nobby, Greig and the others all had problems with him following and stalking them and bollocking them if he caught them out.

Tam also had a hang-up about alcohol. He didn't like us drinking, which was fair enough if we were performing or rehearsing, but his insistence that we didn't imbibe at all was over-zealous to say the least. Again, that was the rule, but we broke it away from Tam's glare. Some said the aversion was due to his father's alcoholism, or that he saw time and time again the more volatile of Edinburgh's youth become violent under the influence in the City's night spots. My take on this goes back to Tam's obsession with control. People are harder to control under the influence of bevy. Simple as that.

Greig followed his brother out of the group and, later, so did Dave Pettigrew and Keith Norman. It was a shame to see Dave the Rave depart. After us Longmuir brothers and Nobby, he was the longest serving band member. He'd been a good musician and a good friend. However, he had been beginning to doubt whether we'd ever make it – join the club, Dave – but that on top of all Tam's rules and regulations, and the relentless gig schedule, caused him to become seriously disillusioned and tired so who can blame him? He also had a girl.

Keith was a lovely fella. Nobby found him playing keyboards with a band called The Images and they palled up. I believe his father was a doctor and that he was trained in classical music. He was very young and had a mournful, little boy lost facial expression that sent the girls crazy. Both in image and substance, he was a valuable addition to the band, although his presence meant we had two keyboard players, Keith and Dave Pettigrew, for a fleeting period.

Some years later, Keith turned up at a naval town where we were playing, Portsmouth perhaps, tapped on our dressing room door and entered. He was doing very well in the Royal Navy and it was a pleasure to see him.

When Keith left, in 1969, a boy called Alan Dunn very briefly joined. He was barely 16 years old and when Tam introduced him, I wasn't sure at first why he had been recruited. He played bass guitar for starters – my instrument – and we didn't need two keyboard players which is what Tam said he'd be playing. It was a strange move. However, Alan was gone in a matter of weeks. I read recently he left because he was beaten up by jealous boyfriends of fans. I really don't remember that, but envious young men had become a problem at our shows.

Too much fighting in the dance halls was a reality of the job. Seeing girls losing control over us seemed to be too much for some of the lads in the audience. It was jealousy, I'm sure, but the boys didn't want to admit that so instead of attacking us they tended to fight each other. It was like they were saying to the girls 'Don't watch them Nancy boys – watch us, we're proper hard'. But they were misreading the girls. They were not turned on by violence and toughness. They wanted smiles and pretty young boys in loud clothes singing songs about love, longing and dancing.

Now and then, though, the gangs did attack us. More than once I have had to clasp my guitar by the neck and use it as a club to stop some dickhead trying to climb on stage to attack Nobby. Or, worse still, me. Some of these idiots thought he was propositioning their girls through our songs – maybe he was. More than once I witnessed Tam stand shoulder to shoulder with our roadies and lay out youth after youth who tried to assail the stage. On most occasions we bolted to the relative safety of the dressing rooms.

Tranent Town Hall was a dodgy venue where we could expect violence. The various gangs would congregate menacingly, and then, mid-performance, launch into each other. The promoter, who was accustomed to it, would then unleash his German Shepherd dog into the melee and then the police would turn up to pick up the pieces – sometimes literally. Shotts, a small mining town in west Lothian was also as rough as they come. The dance hall there was run by a big lump called Colin Baxter and he and Tam often stepped into the middle of a brawl to quell disorder. They both could fight and would stand firm. Haddington was another place we feared.

Tam was very protective of us. I can picture him now carefully ushering us off the stage and then rolling his sleeves up and striding back out into the madness.

A solid addition to the line-up in 1969 to the band was lead guitarist Dave Paton. No relation to Tam, he had been recruited from our now-rivals, The Beachcombers. He was another good-looking boy still in his teens but aspired to develop musically and was already writing songs. Nobby was also writing songs and I nursed ambitions to do the same once we had made it. So, for a few months, at least in 1969–70, it felt like creative juices might flow.

However, as a covers band, there was little or no opportunity to showcase or develop our own material. It wasn't something Tam encouraged. Being a 'covers band' is often a term of dismissal or denigration but everybody had to start out as a covers band. No promoter would book you if you were playing your own material (unless you were established with hit records) and if you tried to sneak them into the set you wouldn't be re-booked. More importantly, the audiences wanted covers and the comfort of the charts. They'd paid good money and would run you out of town if you inflicted your own material on them. The Beatles started out as a covers band, everybody did, and some bands remained cover groups long after their breakthroughs.

We weren't stupid and knew that, to achieve any longevity as a band, you needed creativity. Only success, though, would allow us that luxury. We would worry about that when we had arrived properly. That was how I felt. Our boat was on a firm course to success and I, for one, did not want to rock it.

Eric Manclark was another young laddie recruited by Tam around 1970. This decision confounded the rest of us. Eric was only 16 and couldn't really play an instrument, although Tam had him down for rhythm guitar. We understood Tam's mantra about image and it seemed he was trying to push the average age of the band ever down. I was starting to feel guilty about being 21! But, we felt that our musical strength was being compromised by this headlong dive into the fountain of youth. In his earliest days, Eric just stood there without his guitar plugged in just looking good. And he did look good, Tam certainly thought so, but he was timid. Understandably, as he was only young. He had to be gently nudged on to the stage at first, such was his fear.

Around the same time Tam also brought a lad called Billy Lyall into the band. Billy was about 17 and had been in the Marines. He was a classically trained pianist and could handle a flute, which was a novelty. Unlike some of Tam's other recruits and targets, he was not just a pretty face and I felt he would be musically enhancing for the Rollers. Like Davie Paton, who became his great friend, he was creatively ambitious and was already writing songs.

Nobby, Derek and I all liked Billy – he was a lovely lad. Unusually for the time he was also as close as being out of the closet as one could be in those days. He never said he was homosexual, but we felt that he was – or I did at least. Tam was different with him than he was with the rest of us. He didn't give him the stern talking to about the horror of girls and looked at him differently. Looking back now, I guess Tam fancied him. I have no idea whether the feeling was reciprocated; they would have had to have been extremely careful if it had been. Not only was homosexuality illegal in Scotland but Billy would have been four years under the age of consent while Tam was nearly twice his age. Had they been living 100 miles south, there would not have been any issue as homosexuality in England was legal and the age of consent was 16. I began to wonder about Tam's motives for the first time. I started to think there was something else going on in Tam Paton's head.

In the late 1960s there were no 'gay' people in Edinburgh or in Scotland, even. Of course, there was homosexuality but the word 'gay' had not yet been adapted in this context. The camp TV personality Larry Grayson would warble on about it being a 'gay day' but the first time I remember 'gay' registering with me overtly was hearing Rod Stewart's ground-breaking song *The Killing of Georgie* around 1976: with its mention of Georgie being 'gay'.

This song was the beginning of a real shift in people's attitudes. Rod was giving the boundaries a solid shove. Before 'gay' the names we used to describe homosexuals were far less palatable and sound prehistoric and hurtful now. But they need to be put in context. For Tam, or any other homosexual, to come out at that time would have been risking imprisonment; it would have been unthinkable. Less than a century before, the punishment in Scotland for homosexuality had been the death penalty. In 1889 this was reduced to life imprisonment. It wasn't until 1981 that homosexuality was fully legalised in Scotland, 14 years after the rest of the United Kingdom. In a country where the Bible dictated what was bad or wrong, we were yet to be told that homosexuality wasn't a sin. So, to criticise most of society for holding their attitudes then is as wrong as the attitudes themselves. I say all this merely to provide context.

One night, Tam and I were in Tam's car, driving back from somewhere. I don't remember that we were even talking. Then, out of nowhere his hand arrived on my leg. I thought it was an accident and that he was fumbling for the gearstick, but it stayed put. I looked down. Tam's face remained expressionless, eyes fixed on the road ahead.

'Fuck off, Tam,' I said.

He removed his hand and no more was said. The penny had dropped.

5

Keep on Dancing

AS THE 1970S opened, we were the biggest band in Scotland. Tam had done a sterling job in raising our profile. He was forever placing stories in the press and on the local radio. He paid for coaches from Edinburgh full of screaming girls to come to our outlying gigs which, in turn, created a buzz and soon fans were following us from gig to gig off their own steam. The girls screamed and swooned, mobbed us as we arrived and left gigs and would often follow us in the street. It was exhilarating for us – all this without a hit record, not even a flop record. We still hadn't recorded any music. Now, it wasn't a matter of if we would we release a record, but when.

Tam was always trying to get music industry people interested in us. When, in 1970, he told us that Ronnie Simpson (who was Tam's pal and business associate who helped us a great deal) had persuaded a couple of serious pop music figures to come and watch a gig, we were very excited.

Tony Calder was an impresario, promoter and music entrepreneur. He had partnered Andrew Loog Oldham in his stewardship of The Rolling Stones and was especially good at whipping up controversial news stories that ensured they hogged the front pages of the national press. One story, I remember, was of The Stones urinating up a wall. He gave the pictures to the press and a moralistic outrage in the tabloids followed, coupled with a significant uplift in the Stones' profile. Since then, he had been involved with Immediate Records who were publishing The Small Faces, among others. It was also said (mainly by him) that Calder had single-handedly propelled The Beatles' *Love Me Do* into the charts through orthodox and unorthodox promotion methods. He was still young, not yet 30, a man in a hurry. He wore a suit and tie and glasses with shortish black hair. His looks reminded me of another industry high-flyer – Jonathan King. Little did I know that he, too, would be a part of my life very soon.

Dick Leahy was older, in his mid-30s. He had been steadily working his way up the pop music management ladder. As a former A & R manager of Philips Records he had worked with Dusty Springfield, The Walker Brothers and Dave Dee, Dozy, Beaky, Mick and Tich. He had just assumed the managing directorship of Bell Records UK, a small, perhaps awkward, subsidiary of the giant Columbia Pictures conglomerate. Leahy was poised to make his mark with Bell and the Bay City Rollers would be a big part of his coming success story.

It was a hot, sweaty night in an Edinburgh venue called The Caves that was to us like The Cavern Club was to The Beatles. It was our home turf and the fans really let themselves go. They knew our set well and screamed and shrieked for their favourite numbers. The story goes that Calder and Leahy arrived together and, on the way inside The Caves, they were practically knocked off their feet as charging, shrieking teenage girls pushed maniacally past them in their haste to secure a good vantage point.

Tam told us that Dick Leahy was impressed, saying that he had not ever witnessed that sort of hysteria and adulation with any act he had worked with previously. He was keen to sign us to Bell Records. It was brilliant news. This was what we'd been waiting for. But, there was a complication. Tony Calder, although having accompanied Dick Leahy on their visit, was not working with him and was suggesting we sign to his label. It was not Immediate Records, which by this time had started to run into financial trouble, but another company he had set up with another entrepreneur, David Apps, called Famous Records. We, or Tam, decided to go with Calder. He seemed more flamboyant than the staid and measured Leahy and more importantly bribed us with talk of new amps and advances. We signed for Famous Records and Calder and Apps.

On further examination Famous Records were not at all famous and had no roster as far as we could see. I am not sure what happened between Tam, Leahy and Calder but, shortly after, the contract was transferred to Bell Records. I can only imagine Tony Calder made a turn on the transaction. It was a strange sensation being traded like a street on a Monopoly board, but it was probably for the best for us because nearly 50 years later the surviving Small Faces were still complaining of being deprived of their record royalties from their *Immediate* days.

We left the negotiating of the deals to Tam. We were kids with no experience of business and trusted him to do right by us all. After all, he was a potato magnate. When he explained that we would earn around 5 per cent of record sales it didn't sound much, and we wanted to press for more, but Tam convinced us that to rock the boat would be madness at this crucial point in our careers. A record cost about 9/6d at the time – soon to become 50p under decimal currency – so it represented around 2.5p that should accrue to the band for every single sold. If we were lucky enough to have a million seller, that would translate as £25,000, about £400,000 in today's money. Of course, that would go into the pot to be split six ways. That's how I understood it. Four to five-thousand pounds does not sound life-changing but in 1970 in Scotland the average wage was about £1,500 a year so along with the £5,000 advance we had also been promised it was nevertheless very exciting for us young lads. As far as we were concerned it was a tap being turned on and we'd have lots of hit singles and albums to come, our price for performing would rocket once we'd achieved nationwide success and we'd get writing royalties too.

Around the time that these shenanigans were taking place, in 1971, Davie Paton and Billy Lyall left the group in quick succession taking their talents and promise with them. I cannot deny Nobby, Derek and I took the blow badly. We felt the Rollers were a continuing dispiriting saga of one step forward and two steps back. We felt we were poised for national recognition but both Billy and Davie were frustrated by not being able to showcase their own songs and Tam's over-zealous policing of their private lives. I recall Billy playing the song that would later be released as *Magic* with their next band Pilot to Tam:

'Aw, that's shit', he had said. *Magic* was a great song that has stood the test of time and I'm sure Billy and Davie are very proud of it. Tam missed a trick there, for sure.

Billy flounced out when I called him 'Hotlips'. That was his nickname. I'm not sure if we called him that because he was a flautist or for other reasons. This day he took exception and left the band. He and Davie Paton remained good friends and later formed Pilot and we were destined to meet again in March 1975 where our respective bands' biggest ever hits (*January* and *Bye Bye Baby*) passed each other like ships in the night on the UK Singles charts.

Replacements were quickly found in Neil Henderson and Archie Marr. Neil was a Glaswegian who answered an advertisement placed by Tam. He was a good-looking teenager who could play the guitar well. Archie, we already knew. He was still only 18 but had been in a band called The Tandem who had supported us before and had also been managed by Tam. He came in on keyboards. Ken Stott, the award-winning TV and film actor who starred in *The Hobbit* film trilogy, was for a short spell a member of The Tandem.

It was soon time to go down to London and record a single. We knew everything depended on this. It would be rare to get more than one shot at the charts and we'd seen lots of Edinburgh bands waved off by the fans to the Big Smoke only to come back a few months later with their tails between their legs.

Bell Records had told us that they had hired Jonathan King to produce our first single and this gave us great confidence. King was already an industry figure inasmuch as he had a big hit as a singer with *Everyone's Gone to the Moon* back in 1965. I remember watching him on *Top of the Pops*. It was an unusual, but haunting, slow song perhaps released four years too early. In 1969 not everyone went to the moon, but three American astronauts did. King sat on a stool with his hands placed on his knees wearing a polo-neck and cardigan. It looked like a trainee librarian had wandered into the studio. He was unable to follow the song up chart-wise and therefore became a 'one-hit wonder'. Spurred on, no doubt, by this unwelcome label he became a producer, promoter and impresario. He had apparently discovered the student band Genesis and had many balls in the air. The year 1971 was to be his most fruitful for quite some time.

When he turned up at the Bell Records office in London we all stood up as if a school teacher had entered the room. I recall he asked us to say our names and what instruments we played. As we did he said, 'Very good' and nodded for the next one to speak. King was slightly more flamboyantly dressed than in 1965. He was tall and gangly and carried himself slightly awkwardly. But, with his lopsided grin, he put us at ease and invited us back to his mews house home to listen to some records. As we left Bell's offices that first day, we were told we could help ourselves to any albums that were laying around. We were like kids in a candy shop. I noticed the office girls look at us like: 'Aah, aren't they cute' and the men: 'Are they really old enough for this game?'

Jonathan King was a show-off, self-publicist and that became apparent within the first hour of meeting him. We were practically falling over the names he dropped onto the shag pile carpet. His house was what you would expect from a cross between a pop singer and an aspiring mogul. But, we were in London in the hub of the music business in the pad of the producer of the moment. What was not to like?

I knew, by now, that in the music business these qualities of King were pluses not minuses. You needed to big yourself up. You needed the self-confidence to bowl into record company offices and demand they sign your new band or publish your new song. He played us a composition he had written called *Alright*. It wasn't alright at all and I think the expressions on our faces gave our feelings away.

'Umm,' he said. 'Could be the B-side, that little one.'

He also suggested we choose *Crimson and Clover* as our debut single, an American hit for Tommy James and the Shondells who had recently topped the UK charts with *Mony, Mony*. It struck me as okay but the constant rhyming of words with clover was distracting. The only word I could think of they didn't use was Dover. We liked *We Can Make Music* more. This was a Tommy Roe song. Tommy had recently had a massive hit in the States with *Dizzy* (the song, not the rascal).

However, when he played us *Keep on Dancing*, another US hit this time from 1965, I think we all felt most encouraged. The song had been written by Allen Jones in 1963 but made the Billboard charts in 1965 when it was recorded by The Gentrys. Jones was a respected songwriter, guitarist and producer who later worked with Isaac Hayes, Albert King and many others. The lead singer on The Gentrys' version was a guy called Larry Raspberry. He deserved success for the name alone. *Dancing* was unusual in that it had a false finish: the record reaches a natural end, you reach down to remove it from the turntable and maybe spin it over and it suddenly starts again. I read that this was done first time round simply to achieve the required length of a single by replaying the first minute again. Whatever, it gave it a novel twist.

However, this gimmicky ending caused a problem one night. We were in a dance hall playing on a revolving stage (revolving stages seem to crop up in this book a lot). We sang *Keep on Dancing* and then came the pause. The stage hand dutifully pressed his button just as we had started up again for the real ending and we were spun around playing and singing facing the glittery backdrop.

'What you are playing at!' shouted Neil as our backs turned to the audience.

If I had had the choice I would have selected *We Can Make Music* as our first single as I felt it was more commercial and catchy that *Keep on Dancing*. Shows how much I know.

Jonathan King had hit on a formula, I think. He mined the US for commercial chart hits that didn't succeed over here or indeed were never released here. Under his own name, he had just tickled the top 30 again with *Let It Out (Let It All Hang Out)*, originally a 1967 hit for The Hombres in the USA and *Lazybones* being an old Hoagy Carmichael number.

Next thing we were booked in at the legendary Olympic Studios in Barnes to record *Keep on Dancing* as our new single and King's *Alright* for the B side. King probably knew there were better choices for us than his song on our record but claiming the B side as songwriter would give him a potential income stream should *Dancing* became a success. We would see this time and time again as established songwriters resisted any attempt we made to record our own material and Tam also positively discouraged us from writing anything at all.

Cutting a disc at Olympic Studios was a great honour, the recording equivalent of playing football at Old Trafford or Ibrox (Abbey Road being Wembley). In this studio, The Rolling Stones had made many of their early albums, The Beatles recorded first takes of *All You Need Is Love* and Led Zeppelin most of their studio stuff too. It was hallowed ground indeed.

It was disappointing that Jonathan King did not give us much opportunity to attune ourselves to the tracks in the studio. He said time was at a premium and that he had some session musicians lined up to help. Help was an understatement – they pretty much took over the session. They seemed familiar with *Keep on Dancing* so I wondered if King had been down this road before with this number with some other bands.

However, contrary to some accounts, we *are* on the record. It's Nobby's distinctive voice for sure on the 1971 cut with harmonies from the rest of us. King claims he did all the backing vocals, which is not how I remember it.

King also says in his autobiography that we looked ridiculous when he met us in our 'tartan-edged short trousers' when in actual fact we didn't adopt the tartan look until three years later. He also reveals in his book that he wasn't physically attracted to us. Phew!

The use of session musicians on our records has been thrown back at us over the years as some sort of proof we were an inferior, unworthy bunch of shysters who could not play our instruments.

Firstly, we were boys in an adult world and we did what we were told. Youngsters generally did in those days. We were record company fodder. Studio time was costly. We were a punt and they were not going to expend substantial amounts of money on coaching, developing and honing us.

Secondly, of course, we could play our fucking instruments! If we could not have done so we would have been torn limb from limb in the clubs and pubs of England and Scotland with people wanting their money back.

Thirdly, the widespread use of session musicians was an established industry practice. Were The Rolling Stones or Herman's Hermits a lesser group because a young man called Jimmy Page played session guitar on some of their recordings? Were The Beatles inferior for using Billy Preston from time to time on keyboards? No.

Keep on Dancing was released by Bell Records in June 1971. Dick Leahy's management of the company in the UK was starting to take off. As our record came out *Knock Three Times* by Dawn, published by Bell, was enjoying a six-week run at number one. Dick was also launching David Cassidy over here. Cassidy had made his name in *The Partridge Family* on US TV and was now being packaged as a solo artist. His day was about to arrive.

Gary Glitter, another Bell artist, seemed to have been around for years. We had met him on the club circuit once or twice when he went under the name of Paul Raven. He was now pushing 30 at a time when it was almost a criminal offence to be a pop star over the age of 25, but he delighted everyone for a while with his camp, self-parodying, glitter-based act. We played the Preston Guildhall with Gary later on. They had these stairs that led from the dressing rooms up on to the stage. It was poorly lit and, as you emerged into the spotlight, there was a sign saying Stage Right. Paul was now really and truly Gary Glitter complete with stack shoes, space-suit with huge collar and lapels. He may have had a few drinks in the dressing-room but as his anthem, *Rock and Roll Part 1*, heralded him on stage he took the left hand turning by mistake and tumbled into the orchestra well below the stage. The memory of him clambering back on the stairs, his wig skewed and perching precariously on his head like an exhausted hedge sparrow will always raise a smile.

Dick and ourselves hoped and believed that *Keep on Dancing* would complement the extraordinary run of success Bell was putting together. We sat back and waited for *Dancing* to break the charts. And waited. And waited. Weeks rolled by. Then months. It just wasn't happening. We were getting some radio play but not enough. Even the inventive and insistent Jonathan King could not break it. A review one of us spotted didn't help, saying the song was 'Atrocious, thin and wearying with fake crowd noises'. None of us could understand the public indifference and it was a torrid time. From the buzzing high of coming down to London to see our record company, to meeting Jonathan King and then recording at the fabled Olympic Studios, now we were staring failure in the face. We were not idle, as we had a gig schedule to meet, most of it over the border back home, but our hearts were not in it. We needed a *Top of the Pops* appearance but you weren't considered for that until you had penetrated the Top 50.

Things changed, thankfully, when a guy called Chris Denning left Decca Records and joined Bell and Dick Leahy. Chris had been one of the original disc-jockeys on Radio 1. The national station had been launched by the BBC as a pop music channel to win over the legions of young people committed to the pirate stations like Luxembourg, London and Caroline. Denning worked alongside Tony Blackburn, Kenny Everett and Dave Cash. At Bell, he was placed in a promotional role. He had more sway with his fellow DJs than Jonathan King and, back then, radio play and promotion was the key to a hit record. Radio 1 picked up *Keep on Dancing* and then other stations followed suit.

We were back in Scotland at the tatty shed. Tam had been getting phone calls from Jonathan King. He assured us things were moving. Insiders told him that the record was selling. He had contacts in record shops. People were coming in and asking for it. The excitement was immense. Then one evening the phone rang he asked if we were near a radio. He told us to get close to a set and put on the Radio Luxembourg chart show.

We ran out of the shed and piled into the back of Tam's potato lorry and switched on the radio. Soon we heard the words '...and a new entrant at number 20 is *Keep on Dancing* from the Bay City Rollers'. We went mad jumping up and down and punching the air. God knows what any passers-by may have thought when they saw this driverless, stationary lorry bouncing and shaking one dark September 1971 evening in deep Prestonpans?

6

Don't Let the Music Die

WE WERE BACK down to London in a flash. Our euphoria knew no bounds and we'd been assured that a *Top of the Pops* appearance was now a certainty. We were very hopeful that our debut single would now go to number one. Firstly, we were spirited down to leafy Surrey where Chris Denning, the latest architect of our success, lived in a big gate-house to an even bigger estate, for a party to celebrate our breakthrough. Everybody was taking the credit except the band: Denning, King, Paton. We didn't care though. The feeling that we had arrived was tangible.

The party was our first big taste of celebrity. Robert Stigwood was there. Now Brian Epstein was dead he was probably the biggest manager in the music world. He had managed Cream and the Bee Gees and was, at this time, busy making Andrew Lloyd-Webber and Tim Rice's show *Jesus Christ Superstar* an international phenomenon. He had a bit of a comb-over which put me in mind of Arthur Scargill. Tam was coy in his presence.

A man in a crease-perfect pin-stripe suit complete with waistcoat watch in one pocket made me do a double-take. Smoking a cigarette laconically and holding a cocktail glass in his free hand, he regarded the scene around him with camp detachment. It was Peter Wyngarde who was Jason King in *Department S*. Mike Myers said much later that he based the character of Austin Powers on Peter and I believe it. Peter may have been the first TV star I had met in the flesh. I plucked up courage and went over and spoke to him. We soon found common ground in our mutual love of horses.

Jack Wild, the artful dodger from *Oliver!*, worked the room. He looked incongruous with his button nose, small boyish looks but smoking a fag and knocking back the drink. He was already comfortable in these celebrity circles, I could see that, but I felt a bit protective towards him being so young. Looking him up now as I write I see he was only four years younger than I was, at about 19.

I'll tell you who wasn't represented there – women. The penny dropped completely for me when I saw, on one sofa, two men kissing. The shock of this cannot be underestimated. In 1971 two men kissing in a public place would likely spark a riot. And that's not a joke. The first male kiss on TV was some 20 years away. I caught one of the other band member's eye and we tried not to laugh because we didn't know how to react. We were shocked, embarrassed and a little bit frightened. I noticed how at ease Tam was in this company and any lingering doubts I had about his homosexuality were now banished.

Near Denning's place was a club called The Walton Hop and Chris and Jonathan were keen to take us there. I thought it was going to be something like the Ad Lib club in London and that we may end up chewing the fat with Marc Bolan and the like. The Beatles lived in Surrey, perhaps they'd be there? Instead we were led into what can only be described as a youth club. We were introduced to a guy called Rob Randall who was spinning the records, but Tam, Randall, King and Denning were the only adults present in the back room.

I think we'd been brought down to show us off to the youngsters out on the dance floor; however they were curious but not particularly over-impressed by us. They were mainly skinhead boys and girls wearing Ben Sherman shirts and bleached Levi jeans and braces. They danced to Desmond Dekker, Bob and Marcia and other reggae artists. There was a distinctive West Indian feel with no West Indians present. It was a pleasant enough place, but I couldn't understand why we were there.

Later Jonathan King wrote a song called *Johnny Reggae* and recorded it under the pseudonym The Piglets. He tapped into the look and feel of the Walton Hop clientele talking about 'two-tone tonic strides' and 'real tasty geezers' but naming the main female character of the song Mavis gives away how much he really knew about working-class girls of the 1970s.

A lovely lady from Bell Records called Dinah Knight was tasked with sorting us out sartorially. We went to Savile Row and Harrods to get suited and booted and then to a top hairdresser to be groomed. It was encouraging to see that Bell were investing in us. I hadn't yet cottoned on to the fact that every farthing spent was being charged against our future earnings.

Top of the Pops was a phenomenon. It overlapped briefly with *Ready Steady Go!* but soon outlived it to become a national institution. At its 1970s peak, it was attracting audiences of nearly 20 million. That's almost a third of the country. If you remove babies, toddlers, infants, and people over 40 in cardigans and comfortable shoes – that's practically everyone. It broadcast on a Thursday at 7.25pm, after *Tomorrow's World*, which most people only tolerated because they were waiting for the main event.

I'm not sure if it was this first *TOTP* appearance or a subsequent one where we were introduced to Robin Nash, the producer. He was straight out of central casting with his moustache, bow tie and booming voice. Not unlike Frank Muir, another BBC stalwart. Robin was kind, could see we were green to all this and nervous. He was keen to put us at ease.

People to this day remember iconic *TOTP* moments. Bowie singing *Starman*, his arm draped around Mick Ronson, had a big impact. Boy George, in the pre-trans-gender age, causing parents across the country to gasp 'What is it?' or even 51-year-old Clive Dunn rocking in his chair singing *Granddad* causing most people under 21 to cry 'Switch it over'.

We turned up at the BBC studios in Shepherd's Bush for rehearsals on a Wednesday and then filmed our performance of *Keep on Dancing,* which was to be broadcast the next day, Thursday. Of course, like everyone else, our live performance was us miming to our record. Marc Bolan famously performed on the show with the lead from his guitar running into his trouser pocket. This was Marc's way of saying to the world:

'Yes, I'm fucking miming.'

It was one of those iconic moments I mentioned earlier because rehearsing with us that day was Rod Stewart and The Faces, who then included Ronnie Wood, not yet a Rolling Stone. They mimed to *Maggie May* and kicked footballs around with John Peel somehow getting in on the act. The highlight for me, though, was seeing a member of Pan's People completely in the buff. She didn't bat an eyelid or anything else and smiled at me as if we were passing in the aisles in FineFare. Naturally, we all phoned our parents, families, friends and cats and dogs and told them not to miss *Top of the Pops* the next day.

Those few minutes on national television were game-changing. We were already hugely popular in Edinburgh, and wider Scotland to a lesser degree. Now people all over the UK knew who we were. They weren't chasing us down the street yet, but we experienced national fame for the first time. *Keep on Dancing* crept up the charts, finally peaking at number nine making us a top ten band. All that hard work, all those years criss-crossing the land in clapped-out vans praying the big ends didn't go, all those clubs with their overflowing ash-trays and alcohol-sticky carpets, all those cheap hotels. It all now seemed worth it.

I could devote a chapter to vans. We travelled in them, ate in them and slept in them. Tam did a lot of the driving, to be fair, and suffered the hardship in equal proportion. I'm surprised no musician has ever written a song about the inside of a Ford Transit given that so many spent so much time in them. I remember once when we were playing two gigs a night in the north of England and the fan belt came off. We were on the way to the second gig and we stopped at the side of the road to repair it. It was dark and raining, but we did it. When we arrived on stage in the nick of time we were drenched, hair sticking up and hands covered in grease. In those days we were musicians and car mechanics. If the press had got hold of this information, no doubt they'd have run an exclusive: 'Bay City Rollers Fix Their Own Cars'.

We arrived home as conquering heroes. The fans in Scotland, already devoted and passionate, were now revelling in our success too. Every gig was celebratory in those first weeks after *TOTP* and the chart success of *Keep on Dancing*. The fans felt that they had us first and now they were gifting us to the rest of the country. We were the first Edinburgh band to go down to London and return with a top ten hit and national television exposure. Tam was making hay while the sun shone, feeding stories to the press and radio, sending us into hospitals to visit sick fans – anything and everything.

Around this time, he arranged for us to do some gigs in Northern Ireland. The money must have been good as, barring Lebanon, it was one of the most dangerous places in the world. I expressed some of my reservations to Tam: 'Och. We're not English. We'll be okay.'

A couple of us hid under the seats as we crossed on the ferry. This reduced the fare. Belfast was an eye-opener for sure. Although the 'Troubles' featured on our television news most days, it was a different thing to actually be among the rubble, the murals, the armed soldiers and tanks. Threat and hatred hung thick in the air. It was intimidating and frightening. When we needed to go between various territories in Belfast we were escorted by the Royal Ulster Constabulary and handed over like a hostage exchange to the IRA. It always fascinated me how these two enemies would chat and pass the time of day with each other as we were passed over. Driving through Belfast city centre, Tam pointed to The Europa Hotel.

'I was going to book us in there,' he said. 'But it's the most bombed hotel in the world so I decided against it.'

More likely it was twice the price of the dump he had booked us into.

However, at the actual gigs the crowd went mad, berserk. They loved us, and I think a lot of it had to do with the fact that few other mainland bands ever ventured over. Only at one gig did we experience fear. It was on a later visit. Woody was looking decidedly white on stage and I followed his line of vision. A man, older than the rest of the audience, stood in the crowd looking at us. Every few seconds he'd raise his arm, stretch it straight out with his fingers pointed and imitate firing a gun complete with kickback. To this day we don't know what his problem was, but I don't think my Union Jack socks helped.

One night we had finished a gig in a large club venue. We were having a drink at the bar with the roadies. Tam must have been back at the hotel. The place was shut, and the audience was long gone. A scream pierced the night from outside the back doors. Two gunshots followed and more screaming. Stupidly, but reactively we opened the doors to look. A man was lying on the floor moaning, blood pouring from his legs. Our roadie bundled him into the car and drove him to a hospital. We were told later it was not politically motivated but that the man had been playing around with somebody's wife and this was a knee-capping punishment. Can't say that made us feel any better about it.

My trepidation about touring Ireland was proved correct a few years later, in 1975, when The Miami Showband, a top Dublin group, were lined up and shot dead at a checkpoint on the way home from a gig in County Down. Ulster Volunteer Force members had dressed up as British soldiers and set up a bogus barrier where they ordered the poor laddies out of their van and massacred them.

Back home, the pressure was on straight away to record a follow-up single to *Dancing*. Jonathan King decided it should be *We Can Make Music*, the Tommy Roe song he had played us in his house. The lyrics relied on a lot of 'na, na, na, na, nas' and there was a hint of monotony, but we all agreed it was good enough. We asked Tam to push for us to have a song of our own on the B side but, again, he told us not to argue yet, saying that Jonathan King knew best. King thought it a clever idea to put his own song *Jenny* on. It was a forgettable number, so much so, I have forgotten it. King was delusional about the quality of his own compositions – the bulk of his chart success came from covers, but I think he yearned for his own material to be recognised.

Nobby was very upset with Tam for not standing up to King and insisting our own material was introduced and their relationship began to deteriorate rapidly. Nobby, I'm sure, was also upset with Derek and me for not digging our heels in but we had tasted success after a six-year slog and we believed Tam was right when he said that this was not the right time to alter course.

In the end, *We Can Make Music* couldn't make the charts. It got some radio play and Chris Denning would have been plugging away, but to no avail. We got our second TV appearance this time on the other channel on a show called *Lift Off!*, a knock-off *TOTP* for kids. *Lift Off!* was presented by Ayshea, a beautiful girl who was going out with Roy Wood of The Move and later Wizzard. She shared presenting duties with puppets Ollie Beak (an owl) and Fred Barker (you guessed it, a dog). Yes, it wasn't the most credible of places to showcase our new song, but it was national television and that was not to be sniffed at. More importantly the programme was produced by a lady called Muriel Young who had big successes on children's television, especially *The Five O' Clock Club* which she presented sometimes with American comedian Stubby Kaye. Bert Weedon, he of the fabled guitar training manual, also had regular spots on the show. Muriel must have liked what she saw that day with us and made a mental note.

Sadly, *We Can Make Music* just wasn't good enough. Released in 1972, it had some limited success on the continent but when you looked at what the public were buying – *Without You* by Harry Nilsson and *American Pie* by Don McLean, at numbers one and two respectively – they were meaningful, weighty, durable songs that you just couldn't see ours competing with.

We plummeted into a depression. It's hard to come back from a flop everybody knew that and the footnote in musical history as a 'one-hit wonder' loomed ominously. We knew that Bell may have been starting to have second thoughts about us. Jonathan King certainly was and abandoned what he obviously thought was a sinking ship. By now he had alighted on the band he renamed 10cc and signed them to his label, UK Records. 10cc would become one of the most admired and popular bands of the mid-1970s. They would later write a track called *The Worst Band in the World* and its acerbic lyrics would come to mean a lot to me. The words summed up how I felt about being in the Rollers when we were being accused of being manufactured and inept.

Dick Leahy, to his credit, had not thrown in the towel just yet. As we gigged up and down the country again, already back on the chicken-in-a-basket treadmill, he was searching around for a song for us. Alan Blaikley and Ken Howard were formidable songwriters of the era and, when Tam told us that Dick Leahy had hired them to write our next and third single, we were relieved. Alan and Ken had made their name with the Honeycombs in the mid-1960s. They wrote and produced their number one hit *Have I the Right*. It was a good pop song, but the group are mainly remembered these days for featuring a girl drummer, Honey Lantree, which was very rare then.

Howard and Blaikley were most famous, though, for writing many of Dave Dee, Dozy, Beaky, Mick and Tich's long run of hits. The band suffered, in my opinion, by having that name. It was a gimmick and probably got them noticed but it detracted from people taking them too seriously. They were a solid band from Salisbury in Wiltshire with some good songs – *Bend It,* for example, was a seductive number that used the acceleration and deceleration of the beat to good effect. It also had the most suggestive lyrics I had heard up to that time and I don't know how they got away with it. *The Legend of Xanadu* was another great song and produced one of those iconic *TOTP* memories; who can forget Dave Dee dressed like the Count of Monte Cristo cracking his whip and his spoken narrative mid-song? We toured with them later in our career and they were a great bunch of lads who really did talk in that English country cider twang. The Troggs also had the same accents. God knows what they thought of our Scottish brogue.

It sounds like an urban myth but Dave Dee, as a young rookie policeman before his pop star days, attended a car crash near Chippenham one day in 1960. The accident was bad, and it turned out one of the fatalities was rocker Eddie Cochran and among the injured was Gene Vincent. Both young musicians had been on a package tour of the UK.

Blaikley and Howard had also been writing for a promising young band called The Herd. Peter Frampton was the front man and he was famous for being voted The Face of '68 in *Rave* magazine. He was only 18 then and the girls went wild for him, but Peter harboured big musical ambitions beyond being a teenybopper idol. Two Herd songs written by Blaikley and Howard – *From The Underworld* and *I Don't Want Our Loving To Die* – I felt were quality and ambitious. Now Frampton had left to join up with Steve Marriott, formerly of The Small Faces to form super group Humble Pie and soon they would become one of the biggest British stadium bands touring in America. Later still, in 1976, Frampton, now solo, became briefly the biggest recording star in the world with his *Frampton Comes Alive* album. Another member of the Herd Andy Bown finished up playing for many years with Status Quo. Back, though, to 1972, Blaikley and Howard were probably looking for an outlet for their undoubted creative song-writing talent and to think they'd consider the Rollers was very flattering.

Around this period, during 1972, the band witnessed more upheaval in line-up. Frustration at our possible demise, relationship difficulties in the band and the usual dictatorship issues with Tam were taking their toll again. Eric Manclark left to resume a normal life. Neil Henderson had also had enough (a couple of years later he'd resurface with Middle of the Road, a Scottish band who had enjoyed a good run of chart success in the early 1970s with songs like *Chirpy Chirpy Cheep Cheep, Tweedle Dum, Tweedle Dee* and *Soley, Soley.* Young males of the period generally hold fond memories of the lead singer, Sally Carr, whose hot pants made a big impression). Archie Marr also quit. Over a few months half the band had walked! For anybody else this could have been a fatal blow, but Tam was not fazed. He replaced them in quick succession with John Devine on rhythm guitar and Eric Faulkner on lead guitar. Both lads came from a young respected Edinburgh band named Kip, formerly Sugar.

Tam Paton had apparently been showing an interest in Kip. Perhaps he saw them as a replacement for us in case we had been unable to continue our success. For now, though, he was happy to plunder their membership by taking John and Eric from them, not unlike to the way in which Manchester United would bring in players from a lower league feeder club. We sort of knew Eric was joining us, one way or another, as Tam had him working on the potato lorry a long while before he joined the Rollers. He fitted the bill looks wise, baby-faced and handsome, but he was also a talented guitarist who could play violin and had a keen and broad interest in music for a teenager. Eric had been in the Edinburgh Schools Orchestra and could read music. When Caroline Coon of *Melody Maker* interviewed him a little later she described him thus:

> His chestnut hair has a real shine, his skin is really smooth, his face unspotty, and his nubile beard is shaved perhaps once a week. He is shoeless and bounces around like a jerky out-of-control puppet.

What did she mean, he was unspotty? Is she saying the rest of us were? My first impression was that he was a pleasant boy full of enthusiasm and energy. John was a tall, studious, good-looking lad who could also play.

Meanwhile, Howard and Blaikley had come up with some songs for us. One – *Manana* – stood out. It had a holiday feel to it at a time when ordinary people were jetting off to Spain, and the like, in big numbers for the first time. It had a very agreeable chorus. We all liked it and felt it had top ten written all over it. It was agreed this would be our third single.

Nobby had also written a decent song called *Because I Love You* and Dick Leahy, Tam and Alan and Ken all agreed that this could be the B-side. It felt like a victory. Yet there was more wrangling. It was decided (by Tam) that the 'pot' concept would extend to our song-writing royalties. Tam suggested that royalties should be distributed equally among the band members which was a welcome tacit understanding, I thought, that more of us would be writing in the future and that we'd be recorded. However, he put himself down as a sixth member again. So, in effect, he was taking a management fee of 15 per cent pre-pot (no doubt, generous expenses too) and then benefiting equally from the distribution of money when that distribution came. It left a bad taste in the mouth, especially Nobby's.

Around this time Tam introduced us to Barry Perkins. He was a booking agent and was responsible for getting us gigs. As a chart band Barry said we should be commanding higher fees and getting a better class of gig. Tam believed that we'd reached a level where we needed the services of Barry. He had been involved in pop music management in Manchester and some household names were thrown about. Tam described Barry as our business manager, though that's what we thought Tam's role was. Inevitably, somewhere along the line, Barry and Tam fell out.

Financially, these were crucial times as deals were being struck that would resonate for the rest of our lives. We were youths and vulnerable and were already being eaten alive in London. Tam should have been protecting us, but time would show that he was exploiting us instead. I remember, on several occasions, men in suits coming to us in the dressing-room just before we were about to go on stage. Our nerves were jangling, and our minds focused elsewhere.

'Sign here, lads.'

And we did. Dutifully.

Anticipation was high. We recorded a *TOTP* even though we hadn't made the Top 50 yet. This indicated to us that the BBC thought the record was going to be a smash hit. *Manana* had also been entered into a competition called The Luxembourg Grand Prix International, a sort of Eurovision Song Contest for more contemporary artists. Slade were to perform at the show with us in Luxembourg and, in 1972, they didn't come much bigger than Noddy Holder and the boys. They were to have four number one singles and a number two in this year alone. We watched them in their tank tops, high-up check trousers and stack shoes and thought, who'd wear clothes like that?

We performed the song on stage with a full orchestra. Our detractors would no doubt describe them as session musicians. We were great that night and we won. It was a triumph and our elation was immense. Tam couldn't stop us drinking alcohol at the after-party. I think even he had a wee dram that night.

But it was to be another false dawn. The song made the charts in several European countries but never touched the UK Top 30 – the one that, for us at the time, counted. Beyond the Rollers devotees the song isn't even long forgotten – nobody ever knew it! I listen to it now and still think it a good number and it evokes pleasant memories. It remains a mystery to me – like the attraction of potholing – as to why it failed.

Depressed is not the word. Two good composers produce a perfectly good song and we win a respected contest with it, but we still can't make a hit of it. Would Bell be thinking there is something wrong with the Rollers? Things were taking off for the label in the UK. Gary Glitter was storming the charts, as were his colleagues The Glitter Band but, most of all, David Cassidy was going stratospheric. Schoolgirls across the land were swooning over his ballads (I said ballads) and there was barely a pencil case or school exercise book anywhere without his name scrawled on it. He was neck and neck with The Osmonds in the teen adulation stakes. Dick Leahy could not be blamed if he decided to ditch us now and concentrate on an act that had become the hottest property in pop music.

Was there something wrong with us? Self-doubt, disillusionment, despair was wracking us and some serious discussions between the members about jacking it all in took place. The prospect of plumbing was beginning to take on some allure to me once more. Monotony and manual work sometimes seemed more bearable than these euphoric highs and crashing lows and the constant teasing allure of pop stardom. Even Tam seemed down. We waited for the call from Dick Leahy to inform us that we were being let go.

7

Rebel, Rebel

REMARKABLY, DICK LEAHY still had not given up on us, yet again. He had now hired songwriters Bill Martin and Phil Coulter to write for us. Although, according to Tam, Dick had said we were drinking in the last chance saloon as far as Bell were concerned. This was it now. We dared not put forward any songs of our own or apply any pressure at all. We would do as we were told and go all out for a desperately needed hit record. It had been 18 months since *Keep on Dancing* and we were almost has-beens that never quite were. I could picture myself sitting in a pub, 30 years on, telling some whippersnapper that I used to be in a band. Made the charts. Aye, what were you called, then? Bay City Rollers. Bay City Rollers? Aye. Nae, never heard of them.

Bill Martin was a Glaswegian and Phil Coulter a Northern Irishman. The two came together in the mid-1960s, Bill generally providing the lyrics and Phil the music. Their first big chart hit was *Puppet on a String*, which was recorded by Sandie Shaw. It was entered into the Eurovision Song Contest in 1967 and won it easily. These were in the days when voting in the contest was driven by the quality of the songs rather than political alliances and considerations. The record was also a number one in the UK and Europe. It was catchy pop at its best. Sandie Shaw, who was famous for not wearing shoes on stage, maybe didn't think so. Despite the boon it gave her plateauing career she later said: 'I was instinctively repelled by its sexist drivel and cuckoo-clock tune.'

The following year *Congratulations*, written by Martin and Coulter, was recorded by Cliff Richard, entered for the same competition and finished second. It also topped the charts and has become one of the most famous songs of all time. It's up there in the *Happy Birthday* league – an income stream that will never run dry.

In 1970, they even managed to get the England football team to the number one position with *Back Home*. It was an intuitive title as the England squad, world champions at the time, were soon back home from the World Cup in Mexico after getting knocked out in the quarter-finals.

When we were called into the studios to hear the songs they had been working on, we were very excited. Two, in particular, sounded very good: *Remember*, which was a summery song with twee lyrics that I found myself tapping my fingers and singing in my head long after I left the studio (always a good sign) and *Saturday Night* which was head-turning and jaw-dropping. I remember Derek and me looking at each other, thinking the same thing. It started out with the rhythmic spelling out of S-A-T-U-R-D-A-Y and then went into a rockier, but still, contagious tune. I felt it caught the zeitgeist. At the time football fans were running around the country chanting and chasing each other up back streets and across football pitches, silk scarves tied around their wrists, flared trousers blowing in the wind. *Saturday Night* touched on the amateur and mainly innocent anarchy of all that.

Disappointingly, Bill Martin and Phil Coulter were equally dismissive of our musical abilities at first as Jonathan King. When we came to record the tracks, a team of session musicians had already laid down most of the songs and we weren't allowed to add much beyond vocals and harmonies. We had to learn the songs, of course, because we'd soon be expected to play them live. So, there we were full of hope and confidence again, but our self-esteem under attack by being treated as if we were a cover band covering our own music. Years later, in his autobiography, Bill Martin said that Derek and I were good musicians and the cornerstone of the band. 'They held the Rollers together musically on bass and drums,' he wrote. Sadly, the economics of studio time in 1973 swayed him and Phil into severely limiting our input.

If I thought it was a mystery that nobody bought *Manana*, then the fate of *Saturday Night* in the UK was our Bermuda Triangle. It was released in the early summer of 1973 and was never to be seen again in the UK. A Martin/Coulter song called *Hey C.B.* had been chosen as the B-side. It was a forgettable number about a car chase and ensuing accident – I think. Phil had been involved in the production of a song nearly a decade early called *Terry* by Twinkle, a morbid tale of bikers and death that had nevertheless caught the fatalistic imagination of teenagers and made the charts. It didn't work here.

The apparent failure of *Saturday Night,* and the lack of respect shown to us in the studio, were too much for Nobby Clark and he decided to leave. He had discussed this with Derek and me on a number of occasions and we'd persuaded him to stay. We didn't want to lose Nobby. The three of us were the core of the band and we'd been together now through thick and thin for what seemed like years. However, he was beginning to hate Tam. He detested the London types that were manipulating and trading us like cattle. He had had enough of the failure and knockbacks and didn't like the look of the success if it was to come. He also had a girlfriend who he was serious about and did not see why he had to hide her away and, indeed, barely see her. He was experiencing the usual Roller cocktail of madness. The sad thing was we were on the brink of superstardom, but he didn't know it and neither did we.

Nobby agreed to stay on longer to give Tam time to find a replacement and he was as good as his word. Nobby was, and is, a good man. Derek and I were extremely worried, shuffling band members is one thing but replacing the lead singer is much trickier. The lead singer is normally the main focus of the band. Could The Rolling Stones ever have replaced Mick Jagger? I don't think so. Manfred Mann managed it when they lost Paul Jones and substituted Mike d'Abo, but it is high stakes game and can often be fatal to the band – think The Hollies without Allan Clarke or Queen without Freddie Mercury.

One night Nobby simply didn't turn up and I had to take the lead singing role which I did not relish. To make matters worse the crowd chanted 'We want, Nobby! We want Nobby!' It wasn't good. In Scotland, at least, Nobby was the focal point of the band. Some girls had grown up with him. Our fans in Scotland are die-hard and even to this day grown women approach me and ask how he is. There is a core of them that pine for those simpler Rollers days when we belonged to Edinburgh alone.

Tam Paton didn't seem too alarmed over Nobby's departure. I think he was relieved. Nobby had challenged his authority too many times in his view. His complaining over Bell and our various producers undermining us as musicians (even as people) grated on Tam. He believed Nobby should have been grateful for how far he (Tam) had taken him. That was Tam's ethos. He rarely acknowledged our talent, skills or promise and like to present our success as chiefly a product of his skill and entrepreneurship.

Meanwhile, Dick Leahy, who may not have been aware that Nobby was poised to take the high road, agreed that as we had recorded the song *Remember* in those first Martin and Coulter sessions that despite *Saturday Night* bombing it would be released. It was the very final roll of the dice. Dick made it clear to Tam there would be no further investment in the Bay City Rollers from Bell Records without a hit. We were on a knife-edge. The pot was overdrawn. Tam gave us varying figures of how much the band was in debt, all of them eye-watering. We couldn't understand how this had happened. Tam would brook no argument shooting us down by telling us how it was his funds (or his Mum and Dad's) that were keeping us afloat. Being financially immature, we took what we were told as gospel. I have no doubt that if *Remember* had failed we'd have wound the band up. The end of the Roller road was on the horizon.

Remember is these days often recalled for its 'infantile' lyrics. Critics took the piss out of the opening line, particularly:

'Shimmy, shammy, shong/ We used to make up songs/ Remember, Sha la la la loo'

I never understood the opprobrium the lyrics provoked. It was unashamed sing-a-long, easy listening pop. *Sha La La La La La Lee* by The Small Faces (written by Kenny Lynch) escapes such vitriol and if we are getting on to the subject of inane lyrics Marc Bolan's T. Rex delighted in them and he was lauded for it.

The public, god bless them, liked *Remember*. It was released at the end of 1973 and finally entered the charts in February of 1974 following a mailing campaign by Tam to all and sundry, including the members of David Cassidy's fan club. Tam was proud he had got hold of this particular mailing list and, if true, it was a great ruse. On the other hand, Tam was a master of rewriting history to accentuate his own achievements and role in things. He needed people to appreciate that he was the puppet master and felt threatened when others, such as Bill Martin and Dick Leahy, had a real hand in our destiny.

Remember was a relative slow burner entering the Top 50 at 47, then clambering to 38, then jumping to 18, then rocketing to eight and peaking at six. It then exited slowly enjoying a 12-week chart run to the end of April 1974. It was a torrid time nationally. Edward Heath, the Conservative Prime Minister, failed to form a government in the February and the following month Harold Wilson's Labour Party were able to cobble one together. These political machinations were being played out against a backdrop of recessions, three-day weeks, miners' strikes, power-cuts and terrorism in Northern Ireland and the mainland. Candles were outselling carrots. There was an air of desolation and despair. Those who had lived through the Second World War, drew parallels. And then the Bay City Rollers appeared among the tumbleweed, shimmying, shammying and shonging like flowers in a skip.

Remember began its ascent as Nobby left. The situation led to comparisons with Pete Best and The Beatles when observers looked back in retrospect. It was not like that. Pete Best was removed at John Lennon's behest, allegedly, just before they hit the big time and was replaced by Ringo Starr. Nobby went of his own accord.

So, we had the career-saving hit record on our hands but no lead singer. You couldn't make it up. Tam, I now know, had someone in mind to replace Nobby and one day he brought that someone to the house in Caledonian Road. The 18-year-old boy stood before us had feather-cut hair – half Rod Stewart half David Bowie – a thin nose and small mouth. He was stick thin and dressed in tight-fitting tee-shirt and flares. He was a good-looking youth and visually I could see what Tam saw him in.

'This is Les,' said Tam.

'Leslie Richard McKeown,' the boy corrected him. He had a swagger and attitude and first I thought 'Who's this flash bastard Tam's brought us now?' We went on to a gig where Les was thrown in at the deep end and my respect for him soon rocketed. He had had no real chance to learn any words and was forced to read lyrics off bits of paper stuck on instruments and props, but he did great. His voice had an attractive, confident quality and, even though the 'We Want Nobby' brigade was giving him stick, he glided around the stage confidently, although I knew he was terrified. We knew he was looking for his lines as he moved around the stage, but it was an assured performance. I helped him, singing more than I normally would have to keep the flow. He did great, though. The boy had plenty of bottle.

Leslie Richard McKeown was born in 1955 to parents who had emigrated to Edinburgh from Northern Ireland in the previous decade. Les's Dad was deaf and dumb, following a childhood accident, and sign language was widely used in the family. There were four boys – one of the brothers, Roni, who was a popular disc-jockey in the clubs, I had come across in town. They lived together in Broomhouse, a scheme that attracted Irish migrants. In Les's time, it was rough as hell; you needed to be tough to survive. Even today, they have problems and I read recently that some Pizza Hut drivers were refusing to deliver there. Les attended Forrester School and a couple of years above him was the footballer Graeme Souness, another shrinking violet. Les was a rebel at school and was eventually expelled for detonating a 'shit bomb'. Don't ask.

He left school at 15 and drifted around working in a succession of dead-end jobs, as you do, but he was a music nut, and especially loved Bowie, and nursed ambitions to become a pop star. He finally found his way into a band called Threshold and they must have been kicking up a stir in Edinburgh because they came to Tam's attention despite him being wrapped up and often in London with us. Knowing Nobby was going to leave, Tam must have persuaded Les to cross the threshold to us. I doubt it was a hard decision as we were established, had had one hit disc, a recording contract (just about) and a new song that was showing signs of taking off. Les must have thought all his Hogmanays had come at once.

Any illusions he had of a pop star lifestyle were soon dashed though when we were ensconced in our usual hotel – the Holiday Inn in Slough – when Les ordered a dinner. He ate a couple of mouthfuls and then pushed it away.

'What's wrong with that, Les,' I asked.

'It's shit. I don't like it.'

'Who do you think pays for it?'

Les shrugged.

'We do. It comes oot the pot. Eat it.' He reluctantly picked up his fork and half-heartedly started to eat.

8
Rollin'

THINGS WERE MOVING fast, and, little did I know, they were to speed up and not stop for some years. John Devine left the band in January 1974 just as the sales of *Remember* were picking up. Tam went back to the Edinburgh band Kip, where he had found Eric, to poach young guitarist Stuart Wood, aka Woody, to replace him. Woody was only 16. I remember thinking, 'Blimey, that's making me look very old'. I had nine or ten years on him. Tam must have had similar thoughts and accelerated the river of misinformation about our ages. He knocked four years off me and a couple off everyone else, except Woody because that would have had him at 14 which would have had a sending-boys-up-chimneys feel to it. I liked Stuart from the first day. He was a quiet, polite boy from a good family. His boyish good looks and shy charm very quickly made him a band favourite with a large part of the fan base. With Les and Woody now in place, the band now had what would be known later in the hallowed courts of America as the 'classic line-up'. It is the line-up that most people remember. It is the line-up that conquered the world. It is the line-up that would burn and die.

Meanwhile we had done our second *Top of the Pops* with Les miming to the re-recorded version of *Remember* featuring his voice, not Nobby's. The Les version was now in the shops too, so there were two versions of the same record available. It was all kept quiet. Sadly, I now know that Nobby had travelled down to London at Tam's behest to do that *TOTP* show to help us out and was told it was already in the can with Les. It was a very poor show from Tam.

At the recording session for *Remember* Mark 11, we were introduced to the follow-up single from Martin and Coulter, *Shang-A-Lang*, and we re-recorded *Saturday Night* while we were at it. I don't think anybody was considering re-releasing it, but I guess vague plans for an album were forming and the producers wanted to keep things consistent vocalist wise. *Shang-A-Lang* was a fantastic song. I knew straight away that it was a hit, possibly a number one. For me, it had everything: a buoyant, fun pop song with a great beat and chorus that people couldn't help but hum or whistle. It also touched on gangs, juke boxes, blue suede shoes, dancing and rocking. It could have come out of the Brill Building, the New York song-writing factory, that ten years earlier had produced *Up on the Roof*, *Will You Still Love Me Tomorrow*, *Spanish Harlem* and scores of others. Bill Martin has said that was his intention.

There have been several reasons put forward as to what *Shang-A-Lang* actually means. Bill has said he wanted to emulate the clanging noises of Glasgow's shipyards, but Judy Garland had beaten him to it by using 'clang clang' in a song. He also said that Shang-A-Lang was a substitute swear word that he had used as a kid. For example, when his mother told him off, he told her 'Aw, Shang-A-Lang' instead of something like a phrase ending in 'off'. Who knows? It may have been because he found something that rhymed with gang. Perhaps it didn't go unnoticed by Bill and Phil that Mr Glitter did well with his rousing *Do You Wanna Be in My Gang*?

Bill Martin has also said he was referencing the Glasgow gangs, too. We knew all about gangs from Scotland. It was part of Scottish street life back then. Glasgow razor gangs, real or imagined, had been sending the tabloid press into apoplexy since the war. Indeed, some people thought we were a street gang. Yes, during our formative years graffiti declaring 'B C R' started appearing on walls around Edinburgh and some people believed this was the graffiti tag of a fearsome street gang. It was in reality Tam sending some young zoomer out at night with a spray can. It was an unsubtle way of spreading the word about us like he did with the David Cassidy fan club list he 'found' years later. You can imagine it. Two Edinburgh laddies in the park:

'Are you in the BCR?'

'What's the BCR?'

'What's the BCR! They're a gang, pal. Right nasty gang. They come oot at night dressed in short trousers and yellow and black stripy socks. If they catch you, they throttle you with a silk scarf until yer eyes explode...'

Some years later, when we were more famous, Tam sent us out, by then all in our tartan, with soapy water and brushes to clean off the graffiti or, at least, pretend we were. Of course, he rang the press to make sure they recorded it all for the newspapers the next day.

Shang-A-Lang, the song, has stood the test of time. In fact, a very prominent person when collecting his MBE recently from Buckingham Palace called for it to be made the Scottish national anthem. He described the incumbent one, *Flower of Scotland*, as a dirge. That person was Bill Martin.

Shang smashed the charts. This time there was no waiting around or biting of fingernails. The song was a hit. It might even have flown to the number one spot had it not been for The Rubettes with their song *Sugar Baby Love*. The Rubettes were the opposite of us: they had been made up of session musicians, brought together by John Richardson. The band Show-addywaddy had turned down *Sugar Baby Love* initially, and the Rubettes recorded, and then were brought together by, that song. They went on to enjoy a long and successful career. John Richardson is now a Hare Krishna devotee and goes by the name of Jayadev.

To give a flavour of the charts at the time, behind us was Sparks with *This Town Ain't Big Enough For The Both Of Us* and, just slipping down the from top twenty, ABBA with their breakthrough Eurovision Song Contest winner, hit *Waterloo*. We'd soon meet ABBA and they seemed a decent and happy pair of couples. Like us, they had suffered from being considered to be musically lacking for many years. If you had friends coming around to dinner you'd stuff your ABBA LPs behind a cushion. They were the by-word for naff but a decade or two later they were allowed out of the closet and the public opinion shifted. ABBA were brilliant and supremely talented. *Dancing Queen* and *Take a Chance on Me* are classic songs. The fickleness of taste.

Over in the album charts, Rick Wakeman, formerly of the rock band Yes, was number one with *Journey to the Centre of the Earth*. The success of this album illustrates the chasm in music at the time. Us, The Rubettes, Wizzard, Sweet, Slade, Mud etc all straddled the pop to bubble gum genres, to use an ancient term, and Rick, Pink Floyd, Deep Purple and the gang were the banner bearers of rock, progressive, intellectual and heavy music styles. The divide was big. You'd see us on *TOTP* and them on *The Old Grey Whistle Test*. You needed O Levels to appreciate one genre and spirit levels the other, or so we were told. The music press, now dominated by *New Musical Express* (NME), *Melody Maker* and *Sounds*, covered them, not us, even though our combined record sales were often higher. Even if people liked our brand of music, often they would pretend not to – such was the stigma in some quarters.

While the national tabloid press adored us (at the beginning, at least), using our images and the growing manic fan reaction to sell papers, the 'serious' music press detested us and everything that they decided we stood for. If they deigned to review our records it was only to tear them apart. We were not worthy of measured consideration although (or because) we were at the top of charts, on the covers of every teen magazine, quite literally trend-setting and igniting teenage riots wherever we went.

Caroline Coon, then working for the *Melody Maker*, was an exception to the rule. She wrote a very positive article about us in 1975 when the hysteria was at its peak. I remember we all read it and felt the barrier had been penetrated. Recently she told me about the battle she faced to get the *MM* to recognise us:

> I thought the Bay City Rollers were great, with definite socio-cultural significance for teenagers and pop music – my insight and understanding was against the grain of the macho, orthodox, denigration of 'boy bands' and pop music at the time. I was a lone voice, and it was only my genuine enthusiasm and status as a writer that enabled me to persuade the editor of *Melody Maker* to give me space in the paper for a group such as the Bay City Rollers – something the *MM* had never done before.

Eric was responsible for the next move that was as key as almost anything else in propelling us forward. We had the songs, we had the looks (I'm told), we had the classic line-up and next we would have the style. Ever since Nobby had started making clothes for us, banishing the cabaret bow tie and straitjacket design for ever, we'd been experimenting with our own styles, but it was not uniform. Our haircuts were already gravitating towards 'bog brush' or 'Tufty' styles.

Eric had seen a letter from a fan who had drawn some diagrams of clothing she thought he should wear. This included tartan-edged, riding-up-the-leg trousers and shirts. He showed us and Tam. We could all see something in it. He enhanced the drawings and added more. We had some clothes made and the tartan look developed rapidly. The silk scarves tied around our wrists was a look borrowed from the football fans who were marauding across the country courtesy of football special trains and subsidised by Persil vouchers. The loud, coloured and striped socks and braces pinched from Slade, who had nicked it themselves from the original skinhead movement some four years before. There was a touch of *Clockwork Orange* in there. The high-up flared bright coloured trousers looked ridiculous and if any male youth had worn them down a provincial high street he'd be chased out of town by a baying mob, but somehow we got away with it.

It certainly gave the band a uniform identity. We were celebrating our Scottishness. Proud in our tartan. Impossibly young and bursting with happiness at being able to sing *Remember* to young girls. Importantly, it was an easily identifiable, easily replicable style of clothing that probably looked

better on young girls than it did boys. It was a stroke of luck given legs by
Eric's intuition. Considering how naff the tartan look was meant to be, it is
surprising how many people have claimed it was they who had thought of
it. Tam, for one.

I think that the gang thing and the tartan look not only gave us our identity, but it solidified and lit a fire under our fan base. Girls started copying
the tartan look, keeping their mums busy edging their trousers and sleeves
with tartan. They modified their existing clothes to get the style but soon
sweat shops across the world would be churning out ready-made Roller
clothing for these hungry fans.

Young girls had had no voice up until then. Even when Mods and Rockers and skinheads were in vogue, girls were normally seen as mere adjuncts
to boys. Suddenly they had a shared identity and a cause. For a change they
could maraud, run through city centres holding up the traffic, screaming and
shouting – and not a boy in sight. It was liberating and exhilarating for them.
The Rollers gave teenage girls across Britain, and later Europe, the US and
the wider world, a unique identity and strength for the first time. Students
of the feminist movement have ignored the phenomenon probably because
the focal point was a 'boy band', but this was certainly an early example of
young women demonstrating solidarity and making themselves heard.

The building excitement around the band was tinged with sadness. Our
dear Mum died on 29 April 1974; she was only in her 50s. It was a desperately sad time. We had to travel down to London to record *Shang-A-Lang*
for *Top of the Pops* and then rush straight back to Edinburgh for the funeral.
I recently re-watched that *TOTP* clip and you can't tell how much shock
Derek and I were in. It was all so sudden and unexpected. It was such a
shame that Mum didn't live to see us really take off. At least she saw the
start of the big time and she died knowing that all those years practicing
in the front room had paid off. Each subsequent achievement, though, was
bittersweet for Derek and me as Mum wasn't around to see it. Behind the
smiles we were thinking about our mother. She was a good lady who raised
our family well and Derek and our sisters, Betty and Alice, all hold her in our
hearts now and always. I worried about Dad. I thought when things calmed
down I'd take time out and spend time with him. However, it would be quite
some time before things calmed down.

Dick Leahy at Bell Records and Bill Martin and Phil Coulter were
delighted with us and our progress. *Remember* had peaked in February 1974
and *Shang-A-Lang* was released and charted only several weeks later, now
they wanted to release another Martin/Coulter composition – *Summerlove*

Sensation – only weeks later. It was a good enough song (although some critics claimed a likeness to *Shang-A-Lang*), but the haste worried us a tad. It was like Bell didn't believe in our durability and they thought they'd strike while the iron was hot or before the fans realised we weren't very good, after all. There was a sense of being rushed.

In August 1974, *Summerlove Sensation* peaked at number three in the charts. This time we were held at bay from the pole position by The Three Degrees and The Stylistics with *When Will I See You Again* and *You Make Me Feel Brand New*, respectively. The charts were dominated by American artists, us being the only British band in the top seven that week. I think the song and the Rollers caught the mood. It was bleak out there and us summery boys in colourful clothes singing happy-go-lucky tunes provided an antidote to soaring unemployment and inflation, workers striking, Hughie Green, Clive Jenkins and Edward Heath's inane grin.

Despite not yet having a number one, our popularity was growing fast. We were still playing out gigs that had been arranged before *Remember* had charted and girls were turning up in large numbers dressed in tartan and ready for action. The management started planning a real tour, playing bigger venues, and we were also ordered into the studio to make an album. That had been an ambition for a long time and again we were to be disappointed as the process was rushed and sessions musicians were again hired to do most of the groundwork. However, following pressure from all of us, and particularly Eric, we were allowed some of our own material on the album.

Rollin' was released in September 1974, by October it was number one, dislodging Mike Oldfield's *Tubular Bells*. *Bells* was one of Richard Branson's first real successes with his Virgin label and the album is often credited with giving him the financial clout to buy air and train lines in the future. The Rollers outselling Mike Oldfield was considered to have been sacrilege by the record industry press. Vacuous pop music on top of Mike's thoughtful, pensive instrumental masterpiece? Oh no! Pass me the bong, Tarquin. They slated the album.

It was a good LP. Our three recent hits were on there, plus *Saturday Night* whose day was to come. *Be My Baby*, a Phil Spector number we had been playing to appreciative audiences for ages, and *Please Stay*, a Burt Bacharach song, formed the core. Three other new Martin/Coulter songs and four Faulkner/Wood songs made up the rest. It was an achievement getting the Eric and Woody songs on the album because (in theory) the royalties earned would accrue to all of us because of the shared agreement we had. It didn't matter which one of us wrote the songs (only Eric and Woody, so far) – we all shared in the financial benefit. And who said we didn't play our own instruments on the record? I distinctly remember playing accordion on *Ain't It Strange*. By the way, the shit album *Rollin'* stayed in the charts for well over a year.

The momentum continued. *All of Me Loves All of You* was rushed out in October. We were releasing singles every ten weeks. There was no sense of a career being planned just a frenzy to meet the growing demand. *All of Me* was a Bill Martin/Phil Coulter composition that had some nice hooks, but I don't believe was of the same quality of the first three hits. The fact that it only made number four in November at a time when our popularity was rocketing may bear my feeling out. However, the fans loved it and still do. It was kept out of the top three by an up and coming combo called Queen with their flamboyant lead singer Freddie Mercury and with the song *Killer Queen*. They were exactly a year away from dropping *Bohemian Rhapsody*, like an operatic bomb on the world.

On the B side of *All of Me* was a hugely infectious, in your face pop ditty called *The Bump*. If it had been our A side I'm convinced it would have given us our first number one song. As it happened, another Martin/ Coulter connected group, Kenny, brought it out as their A side and made number three. It inspired disco and church hall dancers all over the country to develop a dance that involved couples reversing gently toward each other across the dance floor and then bumping backsides. I imagine many a beautiful relationship started with a bit of a bum tennis back then.

Tam didn't like *All of Me*, and told this to the press, which wouldn't have helped relations with Bill and Phil, I imagine. He said it was sloppy and sentimental and worried about whether the boys in the audience would like it. He even went as far as saying that he'd had bet on it not making number one.

'We need better material,' he concluded. 'I think the boys can write better than that.'

This is an early example of Tam saying what he thought people wanted to hear. These comments were for the benefit of the serious music press, he'd have said something completely different to *Jackie*, the girl's magazine, for example. They were reckless remarks whatever way you look at it. Bill Martin and Phil Coulter's songs had delivered success for us and this was disrespectful and, if he really believed the band could write better songs, he had never fought for them to be recorded or encouraged their development.

As *All of Me Loves All of You* climbed the chart we played at the Rainbow Theatre in London. It was our first high-profile concert venue in the capital. Harry Doherty, writing for *Disc*, captured the moment:

Gushing winds, spacey sound, a thrilling roar from about 3,000 kids, and they were into it. It was the big one for the Bay City Rollers; a gig at London's premiere concert hall – the Rainbow. And they loved every second of it.

All the gimmicks were there – even the DJ urging on the waiting fans with a series of time-wasting utterances. Meanwhile, the kids, (mostly girls, average age 14–15) were going wild in a show of force that certainly indicated that they WERE fans and that the Osmonds have very, very strong competition.

Ten minutes before the Rollers came on stage, hundreds of them tried to rush the stage – but overworked officials managed to keep them back. The entire teenaged audience was on its feet, jumping, shouting, screaming, waving scarves, banners, photographs and any other object that identified with the BCRs.

But the roars when the five idols came on was something else! It was almost deafening, and the entire hall erupted. The opener was *Shang-A-Lang* and it featured not only Leslie McKeown on vocals, but the 3,000 strong BCR chorus.

That was the trend for most of the set, as the lads made their way through familiar numbers like *Keep on Dancing*, *Remember*, *Summer Love Sensation* and *All of Me Loves All of You*. Most of the songs were from the album, plus a few rock 'n' roll standards.

In a more critical tone; the Rollers' sound wasn't the best. McKeown was strong on vocals, but for most of the time, backing vocals could not be heard. There was also occasions when there was a muffled sound instead of the clear, crisp one expected. Whatever happened to the old traditional encore? The fans were begging for one, although they didn't shout for it. More concert experience on the fans' part than anything else. This was one venue when an encore should have occurred.

That said, I doubt very much whether Sunday's audience paid much attention to whether the sound balance was correct, the guitarist was playing the proper chords, or the drummer was beating the right beat. They had the Rollers on stage and that was more than enough for them.

I remember the gig well. Harry grasped the mood perfectly. We were used to screaming girls, by now, but this was something different. They were as one, surging forward like an ocean wave with a manic look in their eyes and there were thousands of them. We were as bewitched as they were; like we were all part of something, something infectious, something uncontrollable, something a little bit scary. After the gig, we were kept in while we could hear the girls outside screaming 'We want the Rollers' whilst trying to bash down the back-stage doors. Eventually, we had to make a run for it with our security guys Wally, Fred and Paddy somehow bundling us into a Rolls Royce.

Harry Doherty could see the naivety of the crowd, and ourselves, that day. We looked like we were loving it and we were. We had set out nearly a decade before to be famous and now we undoubtedly were.

Our nationwide tour dates were set, starting with Birmingham Town Hall on the 18 October. We were going to hit just about every city and large town and, by the end of it, nothing would be the same. Something had pushed Lord Lucan and the Birmingham IRA pub bombings off the front pages and the media had a word for it – Rollermania.

9
Bye Bye Baby

B-A-Y, B-A-Y,
B-A-Y, C-I-T-Y,
With an R-O-double-L, E-R-S,
Bay City Rollers are the best!
Eric, Derek, Woody too,
Alan, Leslie, we love you.

THIS, TO THE tune of *Nick Nack Paddywack, Give a Dog a Bone*, was the chant developed by the fans that took hold on this first tour. That, coupled with the football crowd mantra *We Want The Rollers!* was sweeping the country. Rollermania took everyone by surprise, including us. Someone said the hysteria spread like snowballs rolling down a hillside. By November 1974 even the often sniffy *Melody Maker* had declared us the Kings of Pop, conceding we were a phenomenon that cannot be ignored.

'Their audience is anything between ten and 15, and their enthusiasm can be realistically compared with Hitler's Nuremburg rallies,' *MM* dramatically observed.

The first gig at Birmingham set the tone. We were caught in a traffic jam on the way to the venue. Word of this spread among the fans waiting for us to arrive and they stormed the city centre road network where we were stranded. Police had a hard job restoring order. It has been claimed the whole thing was a publicity stunt orchestrated by Tam – if it was, I was not in on the ruse. In our home town of Edinburgh, the announcer did not expect, when he urged the crowd to take their seats, that they would do so literally. Here, too, the city's Fire Brigade was in on the act, marshalling the crowds. In every town there were scenes that needed police control when tickets went on sale and then outside the venue on the day of the concert and then again inside.

Promoters hadn't seen anything like it. Even when The Beatles and The Stones played to screaming, hysterical girls a decade earlier, the girls, for the large part, stayed in their seats. With us, the girls moved around as a hysterical baying pack abandoning their allocated places and moving as one on the stage. It was scary and there were real concerns someone was going to be seriously hurt. Civic sensibilities were running high.

Tragedy was narrowly averted in Belfast. We were playing the Ulster Hall and the fans were particularly boisterous. I noticed the security looking worried and they were looking up at a balcony in front of us. The girls were jumping up and down as one screaming and shouting. The balcony was visibly moving, and a crack had appeared in the plaster as if an earthquake had struck the building. We stopped playing and the concert was halted. If we hadn't and if the balcony had collapsed it would certainly have resulted in severe injury and possibly death, especially to the fans below who had no idea of the peril above them.

Only six months earlier, Bernadette Whelan, a 14-year-old fan was crushed to death as girl fans surged forward at a David Cassidy concert at White City in London. Nobody wanted anything like that to happen again. Our stage was encircled by burly security men and St John's Ambulance men and women were kept busy in the wings treating hysterical girls. I can remember more than once passing through the backstage areas at a concert where a teenage girl was sitting up on a stretcher, having just been brought round with smelling salts by an ambulance man. I'd smile help-fully, I thought, and the girl would promptly fall backwards fainting again.

The girls would do anything to touch you. Often, they'd lunge forward to kiss you, sometimes heads would collide with the power of a Glasgow kiss. Other more daring girls would go for a grab of the balls and again sometimes the hand came in like a punch. Bruised bollocks are very painful.

Sheryl Garratt, journalist and one-time Rollers fan, explains very well, I think, the new-found camaraderie felt by our followers:

> I don't really remember becoming a fan. The music wasn't ever that important; it was just good to feel part of something. We'd sit in our bedrooms playing records, updating our scrapbooks, and talking about the Rollers. Which was really a way of talking about ourselves: our hopes, fears, ambitions, desires all poured out. I'd never been in a gang before and it was fun.

Sheryl goes on talk about attending a concert at Birmingham Odeon in 1975.

> I'd never talked to total strangers like this before. We discussed our favourite Rollers, admired each other's banners and scarves, and every so often someone would shout out and we'd all join in, at the top of our voices. 'B-A-Y, B-A-Y, B-A-Y C-I-T-Y, and an

R-O-double-L-E-R-S, we love the Bay City Rollers!' No one told us to shut up. No one would have dared.

Inside the Odeon, we stood on our chairs and screamed. I don't remember what the Rollers played or even whether I could hear them over the din; I'd never been that loud, that uninhibited, before. Afterwards, I felt euphoric. It was pure joy. I loved the Rollers, but I also loved my mates and the bus ride and us all being together in our outfits with our banners and badges and scarves.

At East Kilbride, our security was unhappy with the venue's security and made it known: 'We had Mud here last week and there was nae problem,' said the venue manager. He was forced to eat his words when on the night the girls trampled down the barriers and then waded into the startled security men to get to us. We were taken off stage but not before I had the shoes ripped from my feet. Out the back, we ran to a waiting car and, when I got in, I saw my feet were pouring with blood where I had run through broken glass. Being a Bay City Roller was now officially a dangerous occupation.

The fans were extraordinarily persistent and inventive in breaching the security and getting to us. I remember one night I plonked down on my hotel bed exhausted and heard a little growl. A fan crawled out from underneath it. She had a spiky haircut and looked not unlike Woody, but it was clear she was a young woman. She must have crept in when the maid was cleaning and waited for hours. She had a thick Glaswegian accent and fixed her stare on me. She was trembling, but the determination in her was tangible.

'Take me, Alan Longmuir, take me,' she finally said.

I was unsure whether this was an invitation or a threat. In the best practice of *News of The World* investigative reporters, I made my excuses and she left.

One time in Australia, we were trapped in a limousine as girls clambered all over it. We sunk down in our seats as the roof became lower and lower. A claustrophobia sufferer would have had a heart attack. That was one of the times I thought I might die. In Japan, we arrived at a railway station to see thousands of fans crammed onto the platforms and we somehow fought through them to our waiting cars. At one point it was every man for himself and, again, I thought there was a real possibility I'd be trampled to death. We can laugh at about it now but at the time there were situations that were truly perilous, and lives were being risked.

These incidents, although reported sensationally, provoked the tabloid press to shift into moralistic tub-thumping mode. They soon moved the perception from us being the sweet, adorable, boys-next-door to a bunch of reckless Scottish delinquents deliberately provoking vulnerable young girls into uncontrollable and violent hysteria. Various MPs and civil dignitaries were wheeled out to declare we were a menace and/or we wouldn't be allowed to appear or visit their town/village/bowls club. There is an often-repeated claim that questions were asked in Parliament, but a rudimentary search of Hansard online indicates this was not the case.

Meanwhile, with a few notable exceptions, the music trade press remained vitriolic towards the Rollers. I remember a girl coming to interview us from the *New Musical Express*. She came in with an attitude from the start, a pained smile masking the sneer. She obviously had no intention to seriously listen to what we had to say, or to learn something about our history or plans. It was as if we were perpetuating some sort of large-scale fraud on the British public and giving music a bad name:

'Aren't we embarrassed we don't play our own instruments? Do you agree your music is rubbish? Why don't you write your own songs?'

'Elvis Presley doesn't write his own songs – would you take this attitude with him?'

'Are you comparing yourselves to Elvis?'

'No, just making a point.' And so on. I am a very even-tempered person. I take shit in my stride. But this woman made me lose it.

'What exactly have you done with *your* life, Julie?'

The NME were our enemy.

Tam loved our elevation to being a national obsession. We hadn't only broken the pop world, we were national news jostling for front pages with Harold Wilson, Elizabeth Taylor, Richard Burton and Patty Hearst. He got even busier working on our image. His Brian Epstein moment had truly arrived. We were now packaged and presented as clean-living boys. Apparently, we loved milk. Jugs and glasses of the stuff were placed in front of us at press conferences or when journalists visited. I hated milk. I hadn't been able to drink it ever since the day I arrived at the Co-op milk depot one morning as a kid and opened a bottle and swigged it back to quench my thirst. It was curdled! An awful experience that stopped me drinking it neat ever again. But Rollers drank milk, not alcohol. I bet the Milk Marketing Board could not believe their luck – all that money spent on the *Watch Out There's A Humphrey About* and *If It's Energy You Want Milk Delivers* advertising campaigns and now the country's most popular pop group was endorsing it for free. Or were we? Did Tam do a side-deal?

The pretence we had to present to the public was drummed into us: We didn't have girlfriends, we were too busy. Perhaps one day we would when we would when we were in our 30s. We were all also at least a couple of years younger than we really were. We loved each other's company and hung out together. We loved our mums and dads and wanted to buy them houses as soon as we could. Our hobbies were horse-riding (small amount of truth there in my case) and watching old films. It was nonsense and these days most of it would have been disproved in hours, but back then, in 1974 and 1975, it was what everyone wanted to hear. It was the perfect antithesis to the girl-chasing, pill gobbling, alcohol swigging Led Zeppelin. That's where Tam was positioning us, and we had to go along with it.

Paton's obsession with us not being led into temptation heightened the more famous we became. Now the 'classic' line-up was firmly established in the public consciousness, he believed that any more shuffling would be less likely to be tolerated by the fans. He reiterated time and time again that we were not to take girlfriends or indulge in any romantic liaisons whatsoever. To do so would be career suicide, he intimated. Image was what had got us where we were, and image would keep us there. His careful nurturing of that 'good boy' persona was solely responsible for our success, he claimed. Thanks a lot, Tam. He was continuing to peddle the line that we were merely brainless, smiling pawns in a bigger game being played by clever men in suits who knew better than us. It was humiliating and insulting.

He was terrified that one of us, some of us, or all of us would succumb to the overtures of the female fans who threw themselves at us wherever we went. He patrolled our hotel floors like a prison camp guard and instructed others to do the same. Our security attachment grew by the month. Tam hired Don Murfet and his security company to complement the ever-present Wally, Paddy and Fred.

Tam was spooked by a case that made the papers a few years earlier. A member of a chart-topping group was angry at his band-mates after being asked to leave the band. He sold a story to a Sunday tabloid about members (curiously, including himself) taking advantage of fans in hotel rooms, some of whom were alleged to have been underage. It was sordid stuff but how much was true and how much was invective from the unhappy bad member, I don't know, but the exposure did not help the band's career.

When our sister Betty got married in the church that was literally a few doors down from our Caledonian Road family home in 1975, I guess it was the first time I resented the fan intrusion. It was Betty's special day and Derek and I felt guilty that Caledonian Road was cordoned off and hordes of screaming girls had to be held at bay. There were photographers all over the place and they weren't interested in wedding snaps. Betty didn't mind though and when we all adjourned to celebrate at the Taxi Club afterwards the fans turned up outside there too. We went outside, Derek and I, and said if we pose for some photos and sign some autographs would they all then leave and allow us to have some private family time. They did, photographers and fans alike, and it ended up all very civilised.

While all this was going on we were breaking up with Bill Martin and Phil Coulter, our songwriters. We were putting on more pressure to record our own material and they were resisting it. I don't think they put up much of a fight, after all there were plenty of artists chomping at the bit for their material. Phil Coulter told *Disc* magazine:

> I have encouraged the band to involve themselves in writing. It is a very healthy thing that a band can write a percentage of their own material. It adds to their identity with their public and they can identify with what they are performing. One of the problems with the Rollers is that they don't get enough time to work on songs because they're shipping about all over the place on tours.

Phil Coulter was right on that last point certainly, although I don't recall much encouraging on the song-writing front. This time Bell Records and Tam had to listen to us, despite their reservations about our song-writing abilities, because we were already a money machine and they needed that to keep going and us to be placated. Phil Wainman became the compromise solution.

Phil was a drummer by trade and had played with the band that later became Procol Harum. More recently, he had enjoyed a long run of success as a producer with Sweet who were never out of the charts in the early 1970s with a string of hits written by the prolific composers Nicky Chinn and Mike Chapman. Brian Connolly, with his latex suit and peroxide blond hair and fringe squealing out *Ballroom Blitz*, is arguably the visual epitome of the whole glam rock movement. Echoing what was going on between us and Bill Martin and Phil Coulter, Sweet wanted to write their own material so parted company with Chinn and Chapman who at the same time wanted to move into production so parted company with Phil Wainman.

Bell Records asked Phil if he was interested in producing our second album and Phil said yes. It should not have been a hard decision as we were the happening band of the year. Such was the interest in us and the adulation we were receiving we could have released a spoken version of Rudyard Kipling's poem *If* and made number one (actually, Telly Savalas, who played TV detective Kojak, did exactly that later in the year). Dick Leahy, apparently instructed Phil Wainman to produce a hit album where we played on all the songs and should accommodate at least some of our own material.

In early 1975, we were booked into the residential studios at Chipping Norton in Oxfordshire to make the album that would become *Once Upon A Star*. Those few weeks deep in the English countryside were among the happiest of my life.

With no session musicians in sight there was just us five, Phil and Colin Frechter, the musical director brought in by Phil. Colin was a lovely guy. Incredibly patient and knowledgeable, he found time to give us the coaching, advice and encouragement we needed to become a bona-fide studio band. Half the album was to be six songs penned by Eric and Woody, and Phil helped them develop and hone these. The other songs were Phil's compositions along with his writing partner Johnny Goodison. We were a couple of tracks short of an album so *Keep on Dancing* was added. I was given lead vocals on Phil and Johnny's song *Rock 'n' Roll Honeymoon*. It became a fan favourite and I love singing it to this day. It's a track that nods towards our American musical heritage name-checking all-night diners, Carolina and midnight riders. Whenever I sing it the place starts to rock. The fans love it, but it is not a song well-known outside of Rollerworld. Once we'd established most of the tracks for the album, Phil asked us if there were any other numbers, perhaps from our set, that we thought might be good for the album. I suggested one.

I first heard *Bye Bye Baby* in the mid-1960s and fell in love with it. I made some friends in Chingford near London and went down to stay there for a few days. We went out one evening, I think it may have been in a place called Waltham Forest, and watched a band called The Symbols. In their set was *Bye Bye Baby*. It had been a minor hit for them, but I'd never heard it before. I thought it was brilliant, bought the single and returned to Edinburgh and played it to the band. They loved it too and we practiced it and put it in the set almost immediately. It always went down a storm with the fans. I don't think people really realised it, but if you listen to the words it's all about ending an adulterous affair. We thought we sung it well after all these years, but I distinctly remember the shiver travelling down my spine when Phil first played it back to us in Chipping Norton after he had worked his magic laying and re-laying the harmonies. Les's voice is at its best with his spoken intro building up the momentum and Eric's guitar solo is knockout. Derek's drumming underpins it all. The harmonies provide a distinctive feel. It was one of the rare moments when the whole band were united and happy, and we congratulated each other, knowing we were part of something great. Truly great.

I didn't know it then, but *Bye Bye Baby* had been a hit in the US for The Four Seasons in 1965, making number 12 only. It was written by band member Bob Gaudio with his music partner Bob Crewe. Gaudio wrote his first songs at 15-years-old. One of these was *We Wear Short Shorts* which was immortalised in the UK by Freddie and the Dreamers and remembered only for the boys dropping their trousers while singing it. Gaudio moved on from this and that effort may be best forgotten.

The songs that one or other or both wrote are incredible. They include *Beggin, Can't Take My Eyes Off You, December 1963 (Oh, What A Night), Rag Doll, The Sun Ain't Gonna Shine Any More, Silence is Golden* and so many more. It wasn't until I went to see *Jersey Boys* at the theatre in recent times that I realised all this. In the foyer I overheard a couple talking. The girl said: 'I didn't realise they wrote that Bay City Rollers song, *Bye Bye Baby*.'

I wanted to lean in and say, 'Neither did I and am one of the Bay City Rollers' but thought better of it. *Jersey Boys* is a wonderful, uplifting show. By far, the best theatrical production I've ever seen.

During the *Once Upon A Star* recording sessions at Chipping Norton, we were also introduced to a song Phil and Johnny had written called *Give a Little Love*. We laid that down and knew, too, that it was special. It was such an exciting time. When we wrapped up, everyone was on a high. Phil Wainman called Bell Records and spoke to Dick Leahy:

'It's gone very well, Dick. We've got you your next number one and guess what?'

'That's good to hear, Phil. Go on, I can't guess.'

'We've got you the number one to follow that too.'

Mum and Dad on their wedding day, 1944, Aunt Edie and Uncle Arthur on either side.
(© Longmuir family)

With Cousin Sandra, 1948.
(© Longmuir family)

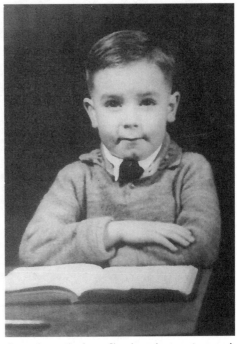

'I was the teacher's pet. She always kept me in a cage.'
Young Alan. (© Longmuir family)

The Longmuir children – Derek and me with
sisters Betty and Alice.
(© Longmuir family)

With cousin Sandra and Neil Porteous.
(© Longmuir family)

Ross Bandstand, Princes Street Gardens, Edinburgh. Our first public appearance was in a talent contest
here. The judges decided we didn't have any. (© Martin Knight)

The Longmuir family home, ground floor,
5 Caledonian Road – Bay City Rollers Central in
the early years. (© Martin Knight)

Inside Ryrie's Bar – a plaque to some
lads. (© Martin Knight)

Ryrie's Bar, Dalry, Edinburgh. I drank here with my Dad. (© Martin Knight)

Obviously I'd discovered Elvis by now.
(© Longmuir family)

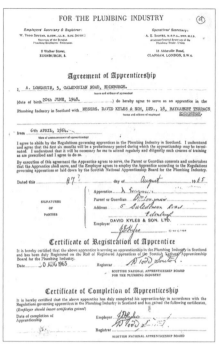

Told you I was a plumber!
(© Longmuir family)

Cousin Neil's wedding. My Rod the Mod phase.
(© Longmuir family)

Ford Transit full of Rollers.
(© Longmuir family)

Me and Neil Henderson.
(© Longmuir family)

Derek Longmuir.
(© Longmuir family)

Nobby Clark, me, Neil Henderson.
(© Longmuir family)

Me, Nobby, Derek and Neil.
(© Longmuir family)

King of the chicken-in-the-basket circuit.
The bow-tie years. (© Longmuir family)

Rollermania. The man on the right clearly uninterested. (© Alamy Images)

Rollermania. They couldn't hear a note we played. (© Alamy Images)

Rollermania. Ecstatic fans lose themselves in the moment. (© Alamy Images)

Rollermania. This fan clearly has good taste. (© PA Images)

Celebrating the first instalment of our hard-earned cash. Still waiting for the second. (© Alamy Images)

I can now hear myself play. In America, 1979. (© Alamy Images)

I've seen Tam in the mirror, maybe that's why I'm not smiling. (© Alamy Images)

I took this photograph of Nobby when we went hitchhiking after I left the group.
(© Longmuir family)

Jake Duncan, our friend and roadie, and me. (© Longmuir family)

Mine host of the Castle Campbell Hotel in
Dollar. Not for long.
(© Longmuir family)

Eileen supporting me, following my stroke, 1997.
(© Longmuir family)

Eileen and I on our wedding day in St Lucia, 1998.
(© Longmuir family)

I Ran With The Gang once more. This time on stage.
(© Liam Rudden)

Woody, Les and me back together again in 2015. It was good while it lasted. (© Chris Haldane)

My lovely house in Dollar. (© Longmuir family)

The life and soul of the party. (© Longmuir family)

My lovely family. From left: Kyle and Ashleigh Rankin, Nik and Carrie Rankin, Eileen and me. The two flower girls are Leah and Lexi Rankin. (© Longmuir family)

My youngest fan, Leah. (© Longmuir family)

Plaque unveiling at Ryrie's in 2016. Graeme Whitehead, Derek, myself and the Lord Provost of Edinburgh.
(© Graeme Whitehead)

10

Rollermania

I CAN'T REMEMBER what I did at Christmas 1974. The days had begun to merge together. The rollercoaster we had willingly boarded was operating at full pelt. At the time, most of our performances were still in the UK but soon a significant amount of our time would be spent on airplanes. We used the travel time to get some sleep as press conferences, photo-shoots, public appearances, TV appearances, radio slots, interviews, gigs and meetings filled our days. Thank God for the milk!

The Rollers diary was full and being controlled by everyone but us. However, if we thought 1974 was lively, 1975 was going to make it look like a year spent at a Buddhist retreat.

At the start of the year we were thrilled to be named Most Popular Group, and Princess Anne, the well-known Olympian, presented the award. She was actually very nice and seemed to know who we were. We were now on the Royal radar. I made a short speech simply because the others were too shy. Until Les, and later Eric, really got into their stride I became a reluctant spokesman for the band. It was only fair, I was the eldest. As any fundamentally shy person will testify public speaking can be terrifying and I was not comfortable. Perhaps it showed. At the party after the Royal prize-giving Barbara Windsor approached us with her autograph book open. Later Gerald Harper, Mr Smooth from TV's *Hadleigh* also appeared and requested signatures. Moments like this, for me, were golden. Lovely, iconic Barbara Windsor from the *Carry On* films was asking me – a plumber from Dalry – for an autograph!

The fan club that operated up at Tam's parents' place in Prestonpans was going great guns. I have seen it written there was 250,000 members at the peak. Tam would play the number up when he wanted to impress and play it down other times in case people thought he was making copious amounts of money from it. I saw it with my own eyes, though. The Post Office had to make special deliveries of the mail. When Eric had a birthday one year it was estimated 25,000 birthday cards turned up in Prestonpans.

The place was drowning in mail. Up to 20 enthusiastic helpers were in and out of Tam's parents' place sorting the mail.

Late in 1974 the Bay City Rollers monthly magazine was launched. I'm pretty sure this came under Tam's fan club fiefdom and was not part of any merchandise deal with an external company or Bell Records. He charged the current day equivalent of £2 a pop which means besotted young girls who were almost certainly still at school and without income beyond pocket money would have to find £24 a year at today's prices. Tam would have got the idea from *The Beatles Monthly* which ran from 1963 to 1969 (and again from 1976 to 2003) and had a peak circulation of 330,000. Even if our magazine was only 30,000, that's close to £1m a year turnover at today's prices. I would guess, in 1975, that at the very least 100,000 were buying it. Where did all that money go? Not to the poor girls who toiled in the club, or us, for sure.

Researching for this book has caused me to think about the money made from the magazine and the fan club. I can remember now that the fan club had a bank account at the local bank. I wonder what happened to the vast amounts of money generated, all of those hundreds of thousands of postal orders?

Also, as part of that research, I have read the magazines for the first time. Tam's fingerprints are all over them. He obviously exercised editorial control and wrote most of the content. Some of it is funny, some cringe worthy, some infuriating. On the surface it was innocent fare for the fans (*How Did Woody Get His Nickname?* Yes, that's a tough one) but underlying this is Tam's voice and ideas. A recurring theme was that Tam Paton was one of the lads, the sixth Roller, who was not interested in squeezing money out of the group – in fact he could have carried on as a very successful band leader, but he gave it all up for the Rollers. According to the magazines, we relied completely on Tam; he lost substantial amounts of his own cash financing the band when it was losing money and that he's been asked to manage other bigger bands, but would never give up on the Rollers. Big London city types may take him for a Scottish bumpkin, but they need to think again. The fan club runs 'at a loss'. Pass me the sick bag.

In March 1975 in advance of the release of the album *Once Upon a Star*, *Bye Bye Baby* was released as a single. We were hoping for an entry straight in at number one. The Beatles had managed this with almost every single in the 1960s and Slade and T. Rex had managed a couple in this decade. Alas, it came in at number eight, but then went to number two and then number one where it stayed for an incredible six weeks. It knocked the aforementioned

Kojak poem off the top spot and kept Sweet with *Fox on the Run*, a song about groupies, from the peak which must have given Phil Wainman some personal satisfaction. We noted that this was Sweet's first self-penned song, after they had canned their Chinn and Chapman song-writing team. *Oh Boy!*, an old Buddy Holly song now re-recorded by Mud, finally dislodged us. *Bye Bye Baby* ended up the bestselling single of 1975.

The song, as interpreted by us, is firmly embedded in popular culture. It became known to a new generation when it featured in the Liam Neeson funeral scene in the ever-popular film *Love Actually*. It was used in the TV adaptation of Zadie Smith's award-winning book *White Teeth*, it even caused a storm (on Twitter, at least) when it was played while a *Coronation Street* character was suffering a miscarriage. We all thought that was in poor taste and said so publicly.

Only recently, while listening to the radio I came across another example, albeit tragic, of how the record has entered people's lives. Back in 1975 a little girl went missing while running an errand in her home town of Rochdale in England. Police put out a description of tiny Lesley Molseed which included the detail that she was wearing Bay City Rollers multi-coloured hooped socks. The 11-year-old was described by police and family as a mad Rollers fan. Sadly, she was found dead near a local layby. A man from the area was convicted of the crime and served 15 years before DNA evidence proved that he could not have been the murderer. It was over 30 years after Lesley's murder that the same DNA technology finally uncovered the real killer and he was convicted and imprisoned. Finally, on receiving some closure, the Molseed family gathered in a local pub. Rollers' songs played in the background as they remembered poor Lesley and then *Bye Bye Baby* came on. The family turned up the volume and all walked into the middle of the pub and danced. They were saying goodbye to Lesley for the last time.

Johnnie Walker, the influential and respected, Radio 1 DJ didn't like the record, though, and he told the world so. He was obliged to play *Bye Bye Baby* as it was number one, but introduced it by saying: 'I can't pretend to like the Bay City Rollers or get excited by the fact that their record is Number One for yet another week. If you really want to know what I think, I'll tell you. I can't stand the Bay City Rollers, I hate that silly little record and I think they're musical garbage.'

There you go. A bit of a furore ensued with Rollers fans jamming BBC switchboards and Walker offering to resign. It raised his profile and probably gave us another week at the top of the chart, so everyone ended up happy.

For non-Roller fans it is the song that defines us. It has crossed over from a successful Rollers' number to one of those songs that belongs to the world. It has a life beyond us or The Four Seasons. I have played it on stage many thousands of times, heard it even more and I still love it. It gives me a warm feeling like it did that first day in Chipping Norton when the studio version was played back to us.

That summer of 1975 was a surreal time. The world was suddenly brighter since more viewers were watching colour televisions than black and white sets for the first time. Someone had switched the lights on. A black man – Arthur Ashe – won Wimbledon tennis for the first time. A woman became leader of the Conservative Party for the first time. West Ham won the FA Cup. Yet, the surreal event that transfixed the nation was an American called Evel Knievel coming to Wembley Stadium to jump over 13 London buses on his motorcycle. Nearly 100,000 people turned up to watch the feat, half willing him to succeed, half wanting to see a fatality. The madman cleared all but one bus and got away with a broken pelvis and hand. Imagine such an event being even mooted today, let alone staged.

Tam booked us into a health farm. The very term was a novelty back then. This was a former stately home in Hampshire years later made famous by being a bolt-hole for troubled footballer George Best. The spin Tam put out was that we were exhausted and needed to nourish our wellbeing. That was true but then why did Tam invite journalists and photographers down every day? It was a story opportunity combined with the convenience of having us under one roof and Tam's vigilance 24-hours a day. The idea was that we ate healthily, did not smoke or drink and subjected ourselves to intense massages. According to Tam's mantra we were all abiding by that regime already. Our skin was exfoliated. I was not aware our skin was foliated in the first place.

We lounged around in fluffy white dressing gowns spotting real celebrities. Tony Curtis and Ava Gardner were in there. Not as an item. Curtis was not a fan of the military regime and nipped out to the pub in the nearby village most nights. There was a story that on a previous visit he had driven his Jensen into the lake in the grounds, Keith Moon style. I saw it as an opportunity for some freedom and I left Paton and the others in there and returned to Edinburgh where I reconnected with friends and breathed in the delicious fumes of a working man's pub.

Meanwhile, also back in early 1975, we started recording a TV series. *Shang-A-Lang* was a half-hour children's slot made by Granada TV. It was the brainchild of producer Muriel Young who had met us a year or so back when we did *Lift Off!*. And, having seen our subsequent rise, pushed for a television format featuring the band. There was some discussion among ourselves as to whether recording a TV series for kids would be a wise career move for the band. But not for long. Derek and I had been fans of the American 'manufactured' pop group The Monkees and they had broken through on the strength of their madcap, half-hour TV shows firmly aimed at children. They showcased their songs and developed on screen the characters of the individual band members. Micky Dolenz was the zany one, Mike Nesmith, the intellectual, shy deep-thinker, Davy Jones, the soppy, love-lorn baby of the group and Peter Tork, the insular, gormless idiot. For a while The Monkees filled the gap left by The Beatles as they retreated to the studio and abandoned live performing.

There were some parallels between us and The Monkees. They too were accused of being musically inept and unable to play their own instruments and sing or write their own songs. They too rebelled against these notions once the initial mania had subsided. Mike Nesmith and Micky Dolenz particularly would later prove they were no slouches creatively.

However, The Monkees *were* a manufactured 'boy band' where as we were not. They were part of a well-laid and executed plan for America to produce something that rivalled The Beatles. Adverts were placed in the media to recruit four lads and, until they met post-selection, they had never encountered each other before. Jones and Dolenz were both child actors. The TV series used The Beatles' film *A Hard Day's Night* as a blueprint. Big name pop song composers such as Neil Diamond, Tommy Boyce, Bobby Hart and Goffin and King were drafted in to supply the songs.

If *Shang-A-Lang* was half as good as *The Monkees* TV show I'd have been happy. It was a different type of show, though, being recorded in Granada's television studios in Manchester with a real teenage audience of girls and a catalogue of celebrity guests. Not much survives as the show went out in the pre-video age but considering none of us had a TV or film background I think it was good. I certainly loved doing it. We were star-struck young men and boys, meeting and working with the likes of Lulu, Cliff, Olivia Newton-John, The Goodies, David Cassidy and Marc Bolan was a thrill. The live audience added a real dimension of authenticity as they surged and screamed around the studio floor. It was anarchic and fun, and I think that came through. It ran for 21 episodes through 1975 and went out on a Tuesday in the late afternoons. Mums could not believe how quickly their daughters were arriving home from school when before they were dawdling home, hanging around shops and chatting with the local boys. The viewing figures were very strong compared to other children's television and, if it wasn't for the fact that the band had bigger fish to fry, there would have been a second series.

We did a show for Granada for Christmas 1975, which we co-hosted with Gilbert O'Sullivan. Gilbert too had started out dressing up as schoolboy in shorts and a cap with his 1970 *Nothing Rhymed* song but had now evolved into a significant song-writer and all-round entertainer. Dressing up as someone younger was not the only thing I had in common with Raymond (his real name). He was also ripped off by the industry. Ray ended up suing his manager Gordon Mills and his record company and many years later would have his day in court and win £7m in damages. We should have borrowed his lawyer. Mills, who co-wrote *It's Not Unusual* for Tom Jones, and O'Sullivan were once great friends and Gilbert's famous song *Clair* was written about Gordon's young daughter.

Although I enjoyed the new challenges thrown up by a TV show, such as learning lines and delivering them to a faceless camera, it did amplify the awkwardness I, personally, was feeling more and more. Here I was a 27-year-old man, masquerading as a grown-up boy of 23. I recall whizzing around the studio on a chopper bike, dressed in school uniform, fixed smile intact, thinking 'Is this right?'. I felt like Jimmy Clitheroe and if you don't remember him try Jimmy Krankie.

One of the TV shows I enjoyed the most was appearing on *The Basil Brush Show* and meeting the fox himself. Some are put off by his upper-class background and demeanour, but I always found him great fun. Off camera he was more irreverent and mischievous that many realise. Of course, a few years later he went off the rails completely and stories of his drinking and drug-taking, often with Sooty's mate Sweep, are legendary. It is rumoured he lost all his teeth bar the front two from excessive cocaine use. I haven't heard from or seen him for many, many years. I hope he is okay.

Following the recording of an episode of *Shang-A-Lang* in June 1975, when Cliff Richard guested, tragedy struck. An off-duty policeman, Denis Williams, who was working as a security guard at the studios in Manchester suffered a heart attack when fans rushed a van they thought contained us (it was Cliff inside who helpfully had agreed to act as a decoy) and later died. It was very sad and we all felt for the family of Mr Williams although it was not clearly established whether the attack was a coincidence related to a pre-existing condition or a result of stress containing the rampant fans. Whatever, it fed into the new narrative that was surfacing in the media that Rollermania was a menace and the Rollers themselves may not be the sweet young boys you thought they were. Tam quickly announced that the takings from the next concert would go to the policeman's family. I hope the money reached them.

The *Daily Express* reacting to the chaotic scenes at concerts up and down the country during a second UK tour which kicked off in April published a leader article demanding some action:

> The hysterical behaviour of young girl fans at the Bay City Rollers pop concerts and the consequent casualties raise in acute form the future of such performances. Either the managers of the group maintain order at their own expense or these concerts must come to an end.

Reading this, Paton would have wet himself with glee. After some particularly lively concerts at Hammersmith Odeon, which resulted in 500 fans requiring some form of medical attention, the Greater London Council announced a new raft of safety measures was being drawn up which could result in us being banned from playing in the capital all together. A GLC spokesman let slip his personal prejudices when adding 'the best thing that could happen to the Bay City Rollers is sudden death'.

A consultant psychiatrist entered the fray:

> Hysteria is classically found in people seeking release, possibly from emotional problems, or among people who have a low boiling point – primitive peoples or young adolescents. The lowest boiling point of all is to be found in a young girl at the age of puberty.
>
> When you condition these girls for weeks in advance with national publicity then they are built up to a release point.
>
> Put the idol objects on a stage in front of them and the emotion that has been built up for weeks or months is bound to be triggered off. It acts as a safety valve – but it is dangerous because so many safety valves are blowing in one place.

Blimey! We seemed to be the cause of everything that was going wrong in the country. Even our peers were getting in on the act. Alvin Stardust chipped in with: 'A pop star owes a certain responsibility to his fans.' Secretly, he'd have given his right leather glove to have had ten per-cent of the following we had.

Arguably, the peak of the madness occurred on a muggy day in May 1975 at a motor-racing venue in Leicestershire called Mallory Park. It was a Radio 1 Fun Day and it was certainly fun – fun walking hand-in-hand with looming disaster. We weren't even down to be playing, we were making a guest appearance to do a radio interview with disc jockey Noel Edmonds. This was before his Mr Blobby days but there was an abundance of Wombles to compensate. The band were to be landed by two helicopters onto an island in the middle of a lake and then we were to get into small boats and sail around the water waving to the fans. Who dreamt that up? It was a recipe for disaster. We flew from Brize Norton military air base in Oxfordshire. What the organisers hadn't banked on was the huge volume of rumbustious Rollers fans that would descend on the venue. Even before we got there, an estimated 50,000 had turned up and the BBC broadcasted an appeal on Radio 1 to entreat further fans not to come to the event. Of course, that had the opposite effect. As soon as we were airlifted in and had boarded our small boats, the place went wild. Girls threw themselves into the lake and started swimming towards the boats. Some of them forgot they couldn't swim. Stewards jumped in to help them. We started pulling girls into safety. Tam nearly went overboard. I saw a Womble wading into the lake to haul one girl to safety. It's a fact of nature that Wombles themselves can't swim.

The security was totally unprepared for how the day was unfolding. Tony Blackburn was speeding up and down on the lake in a speedboat, driven by Uncle Bulgaria (another Womble). John Peel was there and later commented: 'If I live to be 200 years old, I am never going to experience anything like this again in my life. As a cultural event it was almost without parallel in the 20th century.' It was decided we should leave. The helicopter hovered overhead. The sense of bizarre danger was overwhelming. We winched one another into the airborne machine – an act where anyone of us could have been seriously injured or killed– and flew off into the distance leaving bedraggled fans, Wombles and disc jockeys strewn over the site. Disaster was averted; there were some minor injuries and girls being treated for hysteria, but it could have so easily gone the other way. There were fans in a hypnotic state dangerously close to helicopters, I have since had nightmares about decapitations among the whirring blades.

In June 1975, the negative publicity got worse and this time Tam could not kid himself that it was good for the band. Les loved motors and he'd got himself a Ford Mustang once some money was coming in but, tragically, he was involved in an accident back in Edinburgh that resulted in pedestrian 76-year-old Euphemia Clunie being killed. It was an awful time for all concerned. At a later court case, Les was cleared of death by reckless driving but he was ridden with guilt and was in a bad way. The concert in Bristol the following day was cancelled but he was back on stage the next night in Southampton. We all really felt for him. He shouldn't have been there.

One day for grieving and coming to terms with the enormity of the tragedy was considered by someone to be sufficient for an accidental road fatality. During the gig in Southampton, Les broke down in tears, came off stage and then returned, his singing punctuated by sobbing. It was a pathetic and cruel sight. Later, I discovered that Eric was also under tremendous stress that night as his father had been missing for from their family home. Thankfully he was found and had been suffering from memory loss.

A few dates later Les and Eric jumped into the orchestra pit to restrain some security who were in turn restraining a young fan. They felt that the bouncers were going over the top. In the ensuing melee, two photographers were clumped with a microphone stand. The upshot was more negative headlines.

We soon had a feel for how crazy a gig would be in advance. The more working-class the area, the more fanatical and reckless the girls would behave. They'd be uncontrollable in places like Hammersmith, Glasgow and Liverpool but somewhere like Oxford was almost tame in comparison.

Before the road accident, Tam said to me that our record company had been told, by Buckingham Palace, to ask us if we would accept MBEs from the Queen if we were offered them. Tam had indicated that we would. I was sworn to secrecy by Tam but believed this to be true because he seemed genuinely excited which meant, I guess, that he was included in this potential royal recognition too. When Les's accident happened, rather than expressing sympathy for Mrs Clunie or Les he whispered to me, 'Och, we can kiss guidbye to a visit to the Palace'.

11

Inside a Broken Dream

BY THE SUMMER of 1975 the relentless schedule, the fatigue I was feeling and the claustrophobic conditions we lived in were starting to get me down. On the one hand it was exhilarating, we had reached the pinnacle of pop stardom way beyond any of our dreams, but something wasn't right. I believe now that I was becoming depressed. Depression was not a word generally used then to describe a condition. You didn't talk about it. Nobody wanted to hear, and nobody understood it. Not even those of us who suffered with it. You were feeling down. That was it. You couldn't explain it, and you didn't know when it would come and didn't know when it would go. The trivial things became large in my mind. Sometimes, although these wonderful things were happening to us, I wanted to burst out crying. Sometimes, on my own, I did. I couldn't understand it.

I felt awkward in my childish high-up trousers and over-the-top tartan. Having to pretend I was younger than I was made me acutely uncomfortable. Tam had me as being born in 1952. It was a weird situation getting younger on each birthday. I could do with that now. Also, it entailed lying to journalists. When they probed the chronology, some of the cuter journalists worked it out. It meant that if we started the band in 1966 I was fourteen and Derek was 11! At 27 it didn't feel right to have screaming girls of half of my age falling at my feet. Even at my pretend age of 23 I felt too old to be part of what is now called a 'boy band'. I was not a boy and pretending and being treated like I was one often felt unhealthy.

We may dream of being famous and being chased down the street by screaming girls but believe me when the simple things like wandering down the shops or going to the cinema or popping in the pub for a pint become an impossibility you yearn for anonymity. When we were tearing around the world, I was torn between awe and excitement at seeing all these new places and acute homesickness. I yearned for the simple company of my dad and sisters. I fantasised about wandering down the pub with my mates.

I remember being back in Edinburgh one day and I was managing to remain anonymous with a bobble hat and scarf obscuring my face while

Christmas shopping. Of all people, I bumped into Les McKeown's mum in a department store as I shopped for presents for my loved ones.

'Hello, Alan. How are you?'

'I'm fine, Mrs McKeown. You?'

There were no mobile phones but somehow within minutes people were gathering around us. Then girls were tugging at my sleeve. I knew what was coming. I darted to an exit where a boy stood with his bike.

'I'll give you £10 for the bike son.'

It was an old wreck and the boy was delighted and I jumped aboard and pedalled furiously to where I was staying. That's how it was. Hopefully, Les's Mum wasn't ripped to shreds.

We did try and go to the cinema one afternoon. I think it was *Jaws* the boys wanted to see. Little did we know we were already had sharks circling us. We crossed Leicester Square to try and catch the matinee. Silly move. Before we knew it, we were mobbed, and the cinema foyer was being rushed. We decided to beat a retreat to our hotel. How the word travelled so far in this pre-social media age I will never know. Tam's solution was to buy a reel-to-reel projector and we'd watch film after film in our hotel room. From *Dirty Harry* to Bruce Lee to old Hollywood black and white musicals.

Being cooped up in hotels was not healthy. We had to make our own amusement and that normally meant winding one another up and subjecting each other to pranks. Farts and farting became prominent. We rated farts by velocity and smell, secretly hoped the other would misjudge and let loose a wet one. Then we became more daring and rushed to set each other's expulsions alight. This is how one of us came to have a burnt arse. We were young and bored. Farts aside, I also wanted to write songs. It had been an almighty battle to get Eric and Woody's songs listened to let alone accepted. What chance did I have of getting anything of mine over the line? What chance did I have of writing any? When would I see my old mates again? My mum had died, and I'd barely seen her in her final months because Roller business had taken precedence. My Dad wasn't in the best of health I wanted to spend time with him. Time is something you cannot get back. Lost time ends in regret. All this was closing in on me.

We were constantly being told we were rich beyond our wildest dreams and there were signs everywhere this was true. Besides the stark evidence of number one singles, bestselling albums, sold-out tours, TV series, the magazine and the fan club there was the merchandise. The majority of girls across the UK between ten and 16 years old were wearing Rollers' gear. Granted much of it was home-made but a great deal was shop-bought.

The chain stores stocked Roller scarves, hats, gloves, tops and trousers. Woolworths were moving Rollers pen, pencils, keyrings, you name it, by the truckload. Tam and Barry Perkins claimed to be on top of the licensing, but I had my doubts. Even the most competent and sophisticated management would have had trouble controlling it all. Marks & Spencer and C&A were selling their own lines of Roller clothing. These were the two most powerful clothing retailers at the time, with branches in every nook and cranny of the UK. The revenue they generated for a couple of years would have been massive, the licensing royalties significant. Who had it? Where did it go?

Barry Perkins advised us that we would soon have to leave the country to avoid punitive tax rates. Denis Healy, the Labour Chancellor of the Exchequer, was levying a tax rate of 83 pence in the pound on top earners and Barry explained that if we lived abroad we could avoid this. The Rolling Stones had moved to France, he said. It was worrying to think we were losing 83 per cent of our earnings to the taxman but exciting in a way that we were up in that bracket.

The money was not accruing to our personal bank accounts but we all bought cars from the pot, and then Barry Perkins told us to go and buy houses. Go and pick what you want, he said, leave the detail to me. I can picture him now in his glasses, his belly straining the buttons on his shirt and puffing on a big old cigar. He had turned into the archetypal entertainment mogul. A low-grade Lew Grade.

I looked at a couple of posh places in Edinburgh and was then shown a charming rustic property in Dollar, a very small rural town in Clackmannanshire on the road between Stirling and St Andrews. It reminded me of Lasswade where we holidayed as children. It was a detached, largish cottage in several acres of land with stabling for horses and a river running at the bottom of the field. For me it was perfect, and I fell in love. I think I paid £35,000. Derek had tried to buy a house earlier but was thwarted by neighbours who got up a petition protesting about the disturbance having a pop star in the neighbourhood would bring. At Dollar I would have no such issues. There were no neighbours. From the moment I got my hands on it I wanted to live in it, not just own it, but currently that was impossible.

From anodyne hotel rooms, I pined for my new house in Dollar. The fields, the horses, the river at the bottom of the meadow, the little pub in the village. In my head, my few acres in Dollar offered solitude and an escape route from the real madness I was experiencing and the perceived madness in my head. I can remember waking up in hotel rooms and asking the maid where I was. She would answer with the name of the hotel. No, I'd say, which country?

I let my feelings be known to Tam and the others. I said I wanted to leave the band and to retire to Dollar. I was told to hang on for the sake of everyone. We had the second tour. We had the US to break. Big things were afoot. Just a few more months. There will be plenty of time for rest soon. I'd heard that before. Nevertheless, I felt responsible. I'd started the whole charabanc. It was my band. I'd appointed Tam. The other boys needed me. 'You're the peacemaker, Alan. You're the practical joker, Alan. You're a calming influence, Al. You cannae desert Derek, Al.'

The feeling that I couldn't leave them in the lurch weighed heavily and I rode back from my stance. Tam marked this and tried to cement a position I couldn't come back from by putting an article in the Rollers magazine entitled 'Why Alan Had to Stay with The Rollers – How The BCR Fans Persuaded Alan Not to Leave the Group'. That's that then.

Of course, it wasn't just me that was feeling the pressure. We all were and we all reacted in different ways. Some of the band and crew were taking stimulants and tranquilisers, in most cases given to them by Tam, the idea being to assist in regulating sleep patterns, to cope with the punishing schedule. I never fell into this habit, not through any moralistic stance on drugs but I had already discovered mine – alcohol – and by now I was using it regularly. Society, including me, believed alcohol was relatively harmless and fun and we rarely equated it with the powder and pills that were so prevalent in the music industry.

Tam even had the audacity to tell the *Daily Express* about the pill-taking. He was drumming up more hysteria around the second UK tour.

'Two of the boys are on the verge of collapse,' he declared referring to Eric and Les. 'I don't know how much more they can take.'

How much more of what couldn't the boys take, Tam? Pills you are giving them or pressure? Tam went on to say he too was on tranquilisers.

In 1976 there was nearly a tragedy resulting from the pill-popping. Eric took too many sleeping pills in a desperate bid to get some shut-eye. Tam found him comatose and was having difficulty waking him. Eric was not responding. Story has it that Tam rushed to the telephone not to call an ambulance but to alert to the press about a Roller suicide attempt. Only then did he phone the emergency services. Thankfully, Eric was okay and got through it.

I don't know for sure if this story is true. Would even Tam Paton really do that? I believe he may have perpetuated this myth because in his mind and the alternative universe that he was increasingly occupying he felt that this action threw him in a good light. He believed that the people thought what a cool operator that he was seizing a great publicity opportunity that way. Following in the footsteps of Colonel Tom Parker, the shrewd, but ruthless manager of Elvis Presley. The people didn't think that at all. The people thought what a callous bastard you are exploiting a young man in that way.

John Peel, again, cogently commented: 'Whoever is doing their public relations has no sense of shame.'

Paul Gambaccini was less sympathetic to us observing at the same time: 'The Bay City Rollers are a band propelled by publicity, accidents and other people's wishes. Music hardly seems a consideration.' Our lives were being sold off in one-minute parcels. There was no let-up. Paton would point his finger: 'You, you and you – be in the foyer at 6am. You're doing the Tony Blackburn breakfast show in the morning.'

We dragged ourselves from bed to shower to breakfast to limo to studio to magazine office to hotel room for interview to limo to hospital ward to drinks reception to recording studio to record company to bed. Tam would ensure we didn't room together with the same band member for too long in case an alliance was formed.

I remember him bollocking me once in front of the others. He was brandishing a picture of me with a girl at a bus stop. The picture had been taken by a friend of the girl, for the girl who had seen me in the street. Somehow it had got to Tam.

'Who is she?' he fumed.

'I got nae idea.'

'Why are you with her then?'

'She asked me for a photograph.'

Tam ripped the picture up, shook his head and stormed off. I cringe now that I took this shit from this man. My only consolation is that I know that I had girlfriends and girl friends throughout the Rollers' career, so he wasn't that good a policeman.

Once I was banged up in a hotel prior to a performance at the Edinburgh Odeon. I got up at 6am, put some waders on and strode out the hotel. We were being supported that night by a local Edinburgh band. Two of them were lurking around the foyer, not sure why at that hour, and they saw me. They asked me where I was going. I told them I am popping out for a quick dangle down at the Water of Leith. They loved it and came down the river with me and watched in awe as I fished away. I felt sorry for these boys because as they played their set before us their music was drowned out by the fans chanting 'WE WANT THE ROLLERS. WE WANT THE ROLL-ERS'. Not nice for them.

In that summer of 1975, the *Once Upon A Star* album was top of the LP charts. *Give A Little Love* took over as the number one single from Johnny Nash's *Tears on My Pillow*. It had succeeded just as Phil Wainman had predicted. We had also gone back into the Chipping Norton studio and laid down the *Wouldn't You Like It?* album. It was a big departure for us because every song on it except *Give A Little Love* was written by Eric and Woody. I got the lead vocals on *Here Comes That Feeling Again*. We had finally got the creative licence we craved. I think, though, we all privately knew the album wasn't quite as good as *Once Upon A Star* and the fans concurred when it was released just before Christmas. It made number three but only enjoyed a seven-week run in the top 20 albums. It was there and then it was gone. Although it was a fine collection it indicated the first sign of commercial slippage in the UK. Never mind, though, a new, bigger market was being eyed and plans were afoot. Other people were deciding our destiny.

12

Saturday Night

BEHIND THE SCENES corporate machinations had been taking place. A thrusting executive from CBS Records in America had joined Columbia Pictures, owners of Bell Records, our label. His name was Clive Davis, a Brooklyn-born Jewish boy who had made his industry reputation by signing such artists as Janis Joplin, Santana, Billy Joel and Johnny Cash. Davis was an early champion of the album, identifying that artists that could sustain significant album sales were far more valuable to a record company than a predominantly singles act. In 1973 CBS had fired Clive Davis, alleging he had defrauded the company via alleged misuse of his expense account. An ensuing court case dragged on for a couple of years. Columbia Pictures put their faith in him with the remit to create a new force in the music industry. So, in 1974 Clive Davis, aged 42, created Arista Records and to add incentive Columbia granted him 20 per cent of the equity. He was given Bell Records to lay the foundation of Arista and, by the way, Clive, they have a little UK subsidiary you should look at.

In 1975 when Clive had cleared out and freshened up the US Bell roster as it revamped as Arista (he held on to some bloke called Barry Manilow) he got to look at the UK. He could not have failed to have seen what was happening with Rollermania. He has since said that comparisons of us with The Beatles were absurd but acknowledges our pivotal part in the establishment of Arista Records. The easy hit should have been *Bye Bye Baby,* but Clive judged that the American audience were not in the mood for a Four Seasons cover when they still had the real Four Seasons riding high again at that very time with *Who Loves You?* Clive worked his way through the rest of our catalogue and found *Saturday Night* while listening to the *Rollin'* album. He was attracted to its anthemic 'S-A-T-U-R-D-A-Y' hook and its 'melodic sweetly sung verses'. He divined a cheerleader, wholesome American feel to the song.

Deciding to throw the full weight of Arista behind launching the Rollers in America he arranged for us to perform the song by satellite live from the UK and broadcast it on the American TV debut of *Saturday Night Live With*

Howard Cosell which was expected to attract an audience of 80 million viewers. Cosell was a leading and popular sports caster who had covered some of the biggest heavyweight boxing contests of the 1970s and this was his first attempt at an Ed Sullivan type Saturday night variety show.

At this end we played a midnight set at London Weekend Television studios on the South Bank of the River Thames to hit peak US viewing time. Some 500 fans had been allowed in to watch us to add to the authenticity and atmosphere. The television companies got that for sure. The hysterical girls charged the stage breaching the care of their mothers who had been asked to chaperone them because of the late hour. It was pandemonium and Les and Woody were knocked to the floor and trampled in the rush. Les was unhurt but Woody was shaken up and bruised. He was genuinely concussed and had to visit hospital. The American audience, by all accounts, loved the chaos, and comparisons were made with The Beatles' American debut on the Ed Sullivan Show but over here the media went into a fever of righteous indignation. 'THE BAY CITY SCANDAL,' screamed the *Daily Mail*. 'TV chiefs order inquiry into midnight show that ended in a riot'. Les and Woody were seriously injured, the *Mail* claimed. It all happened just as we finished singing *Bye Bye Baby* and the final charge was not witnessed in the US, LWT banned us from appearing live again on their channel. Tony Barrow our press officer and Tam were delighted. Everything had gone to plan.

There is a picture taken at LWT that often crops up. It shows a young, blond girl holding a scarf with my name on it above her head. I like the image, not just because it's me she's supporting, but because she's composed among the chaos but, at the same time, you can see the innocent and earnest devotion. She wanted my attention and she's got it. She captures that moment in time. I like the picture so much I have asked for it to be reproduced on the back cover of the book. I don't know who the girl is. I hope she's had a good life so far. I really do.

The LWT so-called riot took place on the 20 September 1975. The next day our first US album *Bay City Rollers* was released and on the 30th we boarded a plane and flew first class to Kennedy Airport in New York into the maelstrom that had been whipped up. Eleven days earlier nobody in the US had ever heard of us, now landing at the New York airport we were welcomed by hundreds of screaming fans who had managed to lay their hands on tartan clothes and scarves and were chasing us and the crew all around the arrivals hall. With them there was almost an equal number of TV reporters and photographers. It was a scrum with unsuspecting travellers getting pushed and jostled. We were bundled into a large limousine and spirited away to our hotel where even more fans were gathered. I would never make a comparison between us and The Beatles artistically but our reception in the US was the biggest and most intense since the Fab Four I'm sure of that. Phil Wainman was with us and that was his opinion too.

Someone who *was* making comparisons to The Beatles was Sid Bernstein, a music mogul who masterminded the initial Beatles' invasion of America back in 1964. He staged their Carnegie Hall appearance in that year and the legendary Shea Stadium concert the following year. Not only had he set the bar ridiculously high by saying that we would sell out Shea Stadium he declared that the Rollers would be bigger than The Beatles. Sid, you may have gathered, was the impresario who was going to make money from staging our future concerts and tours in the US. This visit was the taster to whip up a storm.

Tam tried to dampen down the expectation a wee bit at a press conference: 'We are not hype. We are the real thing. We've slept in ditches together among the chickens and the cows. What we care about most is each other; our music and our happiness.' Us five boys tried to keep a straight face. Chickens and cows? Press conferences were normally like that: us sitting in a row smiling but scared to say anything off message. We looked to Tam to take the lead. Once, in earlier times, a reporter asked me what car I drove. I paused because at the time I didn't have a car. Tam whispered from the side of his mouth 'a Rolls'.

'A Rolls,' I lied.

I noticed for the first time that even Tam was over-awed. The likes of Bernstein and Davis and the countless other television and music executives made him bristle. Tam Paton felt intimidated. He had been a big fish in a little pond and now he was a small fish over the pond. Sensing he was losing us and control his huge ego could not bear to admit it. He had to pretend it was he calling the shots, he told the *Daily Mail*: 'I feel I have done as much as I can for them. I'm only an image builder and publicist and they don't need that now. Now begins a slow process of me fading out.' If only.

That first week in October, Sid Bernstein had us on a non-stop, whistle-stop tour of public appearances and TV, magazine and radio interviews. We were doing *Howard Cosell* again. This time we emerged from a wrapped tartan gift box. By the end of it we were even more knackered than usual, not even having had the opportunity to adjust to the jet lag. Derek may have been caught off-guard when he told *The New Yorker*:

> Sometimes sleep won't come. I get dog tired and I think I'll be out
> for a week. But I lie in the dark and I can't let go. I keep seeing

the cameras, hearing the same questions. Funny. It's like I'm being grilled or something, like in the old war films. Finally, I drop off, and then it seems I must wake up, start all over again.

Tam would not have approved; a Roller articulating how he *really* felt.

It was a massive thrill for me being in America. New York was like one massive film set. We were staying in the Plaza, later immortalised in *Home Alone*. I felt as if I recognised every street, every tall building from the movies. I expected John Wayne to emerge from a shop doorway, Frank Sinatra to be propping up our bar in the hotel and Lana Turner behind the cosmetics counter in Macy's. New York was the most exciting, exhilarating place I had ever visited. It's a shame we weren't allowed out on our own. We did manage to see the sights, though. Taken up in a helicopter and flown around the twin towers and the Statue of Liberty, ferried around in limos longer than a residential road back in Scotland, photo sessions up the Empire State Building. Photographers Bob Gruen and Danny Fields accompanied us on that first visit and captured those heady, awestruck days on film.

A page boy brought an envelope to my room with my name written on the front in spidery handwriting. I opened it. It was from John Lennon and said something along the lines of 'I'm thrilled for you all. Well done. I'm sorry I am unable to pop over and see you guys, but Yoko is about to give birth. Best of luck, John Beetle.'

And he had drawn a small black beetle next to his signature. I was knocked out. I hadn't even contacted John, but I guess Tam had sent an invitation to John's nearby Dakota Apartments home inviting him over. The perfect photo opportunity. John deciding to reply to the band – not Tam – was John all over. I treasured the letter but sadly have lost it now. It was a casualty of a period of my life when I was moving home regularly, hurriedly packing my belongings into a Co-op supermarket bag. Yes, I know, everybody tells me it would probably fetch tens of thousands now at Sotheby's.

Coincidentally, we were in New York in December 1980 when John Lennon was shot, aged just 40 years. My proximity to the Dakota Apartments and Central Park, where the crackpot murdered him, made the impact even more shocking. I remember being sad when Elvis met his premature end, but when John went it was like being personally bereaved. Maybe that was a generational thing.

The Americans were all over us. We did *The Merv Griffin Show*, *The Dinah Shore Show* and *The Mike Douglas Show* and others, some more than once. Sitting along the sofa smiling and giggling.

'Is it true you only drink milk?'

'And you don't have girlfriends. Is that right?'

All the stock replies. It was all sugary and set-up, but I enjoyed it. We were overdosing on famous people. I shook hands with Muhammad Ali on one of these shows. Didn't realise he was so big and powerful and when he shook my hand I felt he could have crushed it into tiny particles if he had so wished.

The Ann-Margret Show was memorable. Ann-Margret was authentic Hollywood, having starred opposite Elvis Presley in *Viva Las Vegas* and Steve McQueen in *The Cincinnati Kid*. She was stunning then and she dressed up as a Roller and sang *Saturday Night* with us. It's a great clip to watch with an audience packed mainly with old grannies enjoying and joining in with the chant. One holds an ear trumpet and another is knitting. At the beginning there is a little skit where I pretend to come over all bashful in her presence. It was not hard to act that way, but I think it shows how all of us were comfortable on prime-time television. Derek delivers the best line and steals the show. Ann-Margret was delightful, and the show really was as much fun as it looks. Watch the clip on YouTube.

From the US, we squeezed in a trip to Bermuda, another smashing place. Dad must have been loving the postcards. We fantasised about living there. Barry Perkins was asked to check out the tax set-up. We gazed at houses. The world was our oyster. We tore about on motorbikes. Those few carefree days were an oasis in the madness. We were in Bermuda for a reason, back in England there had been a fan competition the winner of which would spend some days with all the Rollers on a luxury holiday. The competition was organised in conjunction with Gales, the honey people, and there is a surreal sequel to this excursion some years ahead.

Back at home, *Money Honey* was released as a single. Written by Eric and Woody, it was the first Rollers' single not to be written by people outside the band. I thought it was a very good, rocky song but a sharp change of gear from *Give a Little Love*. It was funkier and punchier and not our usual melodic, happy-go-lucky, head-swaying fare. We were all nervous about how the fans would react, but they were growing up and we hoped we were growing with them. It ended up making number three with only *You Sexy Thing* by Hot Chocolate and *Trail of the Lonesome Pine* by Laurel and Hardy keeping us from the pinnacle.

I didn't think this was too bad. It was an achievement for Eric and Woody and should have built their confidence higher. Next, they could write something bigger and better and we'd be on course for another phase of our career where we'd develop musically and have some longevity. Unfortunately, Tam was not very complimentary, moaning that the song had broken our run of number ones. *Money Honey* was later released as our second single in the States and went to number nine. Although this didn't match what *Saturday Night* had done there was no sense that things there were going off the boil stateside. In fact, it was the opposite. *Money Honey*, though, was never one that went down as well as some of the others at live concerts.

In November 1975 we played the Empire Pool, Wembley in front of 8,000 fans. Gary Glitter and those pesky Wombles were there again. We were presented with a Best Group award that day by TV chat show host Russell Harty. He was ITV's answer to Michael Parkinson. Backstage he made a few risqué remarks to me and I realised he was gay. Someone with him whispered: 'Mr Harty, really likes you.' I avoided Mr Harty thereafter.

Next up we were on a plane to Australia for some pre-publicity. Tam took just me, Woody and Eric. He was losing confidence in Les as he was losing control. The air gun incident hadn't helped: Les had been accused of firing one from his home and hitting a fan with a pellet. It turned out to be somebody else.

The welcome in Australia when we went to tour was astounding. Fans mobbed us as we landed at regional airports. We sold out two nights in Melbourne, Canberra and other major cities. We were all over the TV. Woody collapsed with exhaustion. I can picture him now laying on a plane between gigs, white as a sheet with a saline drip in his arm. He was 18 and was being dragged around the other side of the world when, really, he should have been at home having a rest in the loving care of his Mum and Dad. Because of Woody's exhaustion and frailty, the New Zealand leg of the tour was postponed.

Saturday Night was released in the US at the end of 1975 and was the first number one of 1976 and it spent a healthy 17 weeks on the chart. Clive Davis had picked *Marlina* as the B side. *Marlina* was from the *Once Upon A Star* album and in my opinion among the best songs Eric and Woody ever wrote. Although, I notice Les is also on the credits, so he must have contributed too. Maybe I'm biased about *Marlina* because it features a stallion. Bill Martin and Phil Coulter's *Saturday Night* composition had finally got the recognition it deserved well over two years after we first recorded it back in the days of Nobby. That all seemed so long ago. If *Bye Bye Baby* defines us in the UK, *Saturday Night* does the same in America.

Was this the pinnacle of our achievement? Being number one in America in January of 1976? I think so. In the biggest economy and democracy in the world we were riding high. Everybody was talking about us and Rollermania had ignited. We had moved to another level.

13
The Way I Feel Tonight

WHILE THE BAY City Rollers were scaling the heights, I was plumbing the depths. Excuse the pun. My depression and disillusionment had returned with a vengeance. I was deeply unhappy. I just wanted to retreat to Dollar, spend time with my old dad, drink beer in the pub with friends, take my rod down to the river and fish for trout. I wanted to ride my horse across the fields and down the tracks, and to go to bed and sleep. I didn't want to hear a popping camera or alarm clock again. No more inane grinning for the press when answering stupid questions. I wanted to stop pretending that I liked milk and give up the ridiculous façade of not wanting a girlfriend. Tam Paton was suffocating me.

The lads, too, were getting me down. They were rowing constantly, Eric and Les mainly. They had a personality clash and differed over the direction of the band. Eric wanted to move the band further away from its overtly commercial, teenybopper anchor while Les was wary. Eric wanted to do more of his songs, Les wanted less of them. I wanted to do my songs, but nobody piped up about them, not even me. I hadn't written them yet. Woody backed Eric up on most things and Derek was stuck in the middle. I, most of the time, acted as peacemaker trying to make light of things, trying to find a way forward. Placating everyone. I was sick of that, too. We were all sick of each other. Not surprising seeing that we had been cocooned together for years. I decided for the second time to leave the band. This time I would not be dissuaded.

As far as I was concerned, I was sitting on untold riches and that influenced the decision. Hopping into limos, flopping down in five-star hotels, boarding first class on jets gives you that mindset. We were on the news on TV on both sides of the Atlantic. If one of us belched it was written up by the press. Our records were everywhere, and a significant demographic of the population were dressing like us. There was absolutely no doubt that the Rollers industry had and still was generating millions each week. I was not a greedy man. All I needed was my house, my car and most importantly my time. There would be enough money for that, surely? I was happy for the boys to carry on without me. I wished them every success. To me one million pounds was not much different from ten million pounds. In a strange way I didn't want too much. I sort of knew it might weigh on me. A US tour, a third UK tour, a Canada tour, a new album all stretched out in front of me. I could see no end to the madness. No respite. And I was still walking around like a man going to a fancy-dress party dressed as Dennis the Menace.

One of the final triggers was when I was back at home. I used to hide out at my uncle Arthur's house, on Lauriston Place, which was a fan-free zone. They didn't know about it. Somehow Tam worked out I was there. He turned up and banged on the door.

'Is Alan in there?'

My uncle told him I wasn't. Tam looked over his shoulder disbelievingly. 'He's not here.'

He was behaving like John Thaw in *The Sweeney*. More so because he then sat outside in his car stalking the house. I'm sure Eric and Woody were sitting in the back.

At Uncle Arthur's, I bathed in the simple life. I craved childhood familiarity. We'd sit, a bunch of us, family and friends, *Grandstand* on the TV, playing cards. In the evening we'd wander down to the Railway Club. Mum had played Bingo in here. Men sat around playing dominoes. Foaming pints were carried to tables. The banter was always top quality. I just ached to have this life again.

I walked into Tam's office and resigned. I told him that he showed no respect for me, or the band. He was mad, pissed off that he had not sacked me first. He didn't try and talk me out of it. Far from it. He insisted that I co-operated with the 'transition' as he called it. He wanted me to tell the press I was retiring because I felt too old and it was time to make way for younger blood. That was the official line. I was not to talk to the media or dispute his version of events. I agreed. I just wanted out and would have agreed to him telling the world I was having a sex change if that's what it took. He walked straight out of the office and told the others that he'd sacked me. Again, the ego took precedence. He could not bear to admit that one of 'his' boys had decided something for himself. That someone had defied him. Remember, Tam Paton could not fire me. It was *my* band.

A campaign of misinformation ensued. Paton started painting me as unstable. It suited the narrative that only someone who was having problems in the head would want to leave the greatest group in the world. He was briefing the press 'off the record' that I had made some suicide attempts. Naturally, this speculation was printed and there was even examples of direct quotes from me admitting suicidal behaviour. One of the stories was that I had put my head in the gas oven at home at Caledonian Road. Another was that I had taken an overdose and staggered out the house in Dollar down to the stable and laid down to die in the hay with my beloved horse beside me. My trusty stable lad found me and phoned an ambulance.

They were complete fabrications. The kitchen at Caledonian Road was the busiest room in the house. You can picture it.

Dad: 'What are you doing down there, son. Kneeling with your head in the oven.'

Me: 'Aw nothing Dad. Just scraping a bit of old shepherd's pie oot here.'

And as far as the overdose goes. I never had a stable lad. Trusty or not. Now, someone may have once (or twice) found me pissed having a kip somewhere on the land around my house. But that's a different story.

The relief of quitting was palpable. To own my time again was a bigger buzz at first than appearing on prime-time American television. It's amazing the simple pleasure that can be derived from simple pleasures. I remember walking down to the river alone, early one morning, stripping naked and jumping in and swimming. I was soon doing it regularly. Glorious. I felt free. I spent time in the village pub the Dollar Arms where the locals didn't give two hoots who I was. Nobby Clark even came and joined me and we renewed our friendship. Two ex-Rollers together. Had we have been inclined we could have almost filled the pub with ex-Rollers by then. Nobby and I spent great times getting drunk in Dollar and later hitchhiking and back-packing around the country. I was happy. Dad came to stay, and we bonded once more chopping up wood, feeding the horses, carrying out DIY and having a drink. I even got in the habit of riding my horse to and from the pub to avoid any chance of a drinking and driving charge and the media scrum that would follow. Some industrious fans found me and the occasional press man or woman. But they soon lost interest. Fittingly, I had officially left the band on April Fool's Day 1976. By the summer I was yesterday's news.

Tam Paton made sure of that. He drafted in Ian Mitchell, a young bass guitarist from the band Young City Stars who had supported us a few times. They were from Downpatrick in Northern Ireland, but Tam had brought them to Edinburgh where he was going to try and break them through. Ian was only 17 years old, more than ten years my junior, but he looked even younger. Seriously, he could have passed for 13. Tam was determined to make the transition seamless. I was cajoled into photo-shoots and interviews where I welcomed Ian to the band. 'The band needs an injection of new blood. And Ian is the perfect choice. I've had my day. I'm an old man.' Here's my mantle son, take it. All the bollocks. I didn't care, though, I wanted out badly. I'd have piggy-backed Ian with my buttocks painted tartan up and down Tin Pan Alley for a photo shoot if they asked me.

This charade culminated in a promotional film we made for the single *Love Me Like I Love You* which shows me morphing into Ian. How's that for continuity? I'm standing on a glittery ball with the other four encircling me all looking at me fondly and then the picture fades and in comes Ian in his white tee-shirt, braces and knee-length scarf. Les and company cannot contain their happiness. It's like their little brother has come back with the fags they sent him down the shops for.

I didn't get to know Ian at all then. His youthfulness worried me. I wanted to get hold of him and say 'don't do it' but he was already in the music business and was keen. He and everyone else believed he had been parachuted into the big money. It would have seemed like sour grapes if I had stuck my oar in. Now, I wonder if Tam's pursuit of Ian was purely professional.

Muff Winwood produced *Love Me Like I Love You*. Muff was a respected producer having cut his teeth with The Spencer Davis Group in the 1960s. His little brother Stevie Winwood, also in the group, later formed the early 'supergroups' Traffic and Blind Faith before embarking on a long and successful solo career. I read somewhere that Muff bought himself a cottage in Cornwall on the money he was paid to produce this record. So, the Roller money was getting out to some people.

Love Me Like I Love You was a compromise song from Eric and Woody. It moved away from the more adventurous *Money Honey* back to something more akin to *Give A Little Love* but at least it was written by them. Some self-respect had been clung on to. It made number four in the charts jostling for top three slots with ABBA and Brotherhood of Man. Meanwhile the band, without me, were working on the *Dedication* album, produced by Jimmy Ienner. When it was released in September, it was very well received. Alwyn Turner, the writer and cultural historian, believes it to be the Bay City Rollers' masterpiece.

Dedication featured the next Rollers' single *I Only Want to Be with You*. The song had been written by Mike Hawker and was recorded first by Dusty Springfield who had a top ten hit with it and appeared on the first ever *Top of the Pops* performing it. Mike also wrote *Walking Back to Happiness* and *Don't Treat Me like a Child* for child star Helen Shapiro. I was curious that the boys had reverted to a cover, good as it was, and soon learned that it was Clive Davis's choice. The head of Arista would have been a hard man to resist. Especially now that America was calling the shots on the band's career. *I Only Want to Be with You* made number 12 in the charts over there and number four over here.

I am under no illusions that Clive Davis went to great lengths to break us in America and succeeded gloriously but I never liked the man. I liked Dick Leahy his UK equivalent, but Clive Davis struck me as cold and calculating and he obviously was. That's one of the reasons he has done so well. You need to be tough in business, as well as shrewd. Us Rollers were neither.

Back in Dollar, I had called Tam and asked for my money. It was time to shake out the pot. Obviously, I understood by now that the monies I had received and expenses I had incurred would be set against my share but I was expecting a million or several hundred thousand pounds at worst. Tam said speak to the accountants like it wasn't really his responsibility and that would be his stance going forward. The accountant explained that it wasn't easy as that. Monies had been channelled through offshore companies to minimise tax and they could not just be liquidated. We were a company and it was difficult to pay one without the others. Okay, pay us all then. There were legal and timing issues to consider. Also, there were numerous organisations to deal with – record companies, television companies, tour organisers, licensing agencies. The list was endless, and a quagmire was revealed. I was told to be patient and that the money would be released as soon as was possible. I was kept quiet with an advance on my share. Not a huge amount but enough to keep me going doing nothing and feed the horse.

I had a bad feeling deep inside about it. I didn't suspect wrongdoing so much but I did smell incompetence. I got the impression that Tam and our army of advisers weren't too sure how it all worked. I warned the others. Said I believed Tam had got out of his depth and nobody was really looking after our commercial interests. I know I was no longer in the group, but my money was.

I got a train to London and went to see Bell Records with my concerns. Their retort was that the record company would have paid any monies due, less expenses, it was down to our accountants and advisors to pull it out of the financial web they had created. The other guys had mild concerns too, but things were going great guns still, especially in America. There would be plenty of time when things calmed down to sit down, count the money and divvy it up. I went out into my backyard tipped out a bucket of sand and buried my head in it.

I fell into a leisurely routine in Dollar. It was a bit annoying that everybody thought I was an eccentric multi-millionaire when I had no idea how rich or poor I was. It was the hottest summer of my lifetime. Rivers were drying up. Office workers stripped almost naked in parks. People were being threatened with prison for washing their cars and watering their geraniums. A Minister for Drought was appointed. He couldn't seem to make it rain. Useless man. Elton John and Kiki Dee were number one with a jaunty duet called *Don't Go Breaking My Heart*. Young girls who would have been Bay City Rollers fans a year or two earlier turned their attention to a good looking, lantern-jawed Swede called Björn Borg. He played a bit of tennis and hung out Wimbledon way.

I had met Julie who worked in a nearby stables and we became an item after I bought a horse and bought it to Dollar. We met in the hills around my home, both on horseback. I felt like Heathcliff from *Wuthering Heights*. A love affair developed. Dad spent a lot of precious time with us and we all spent a lot of time in the pub. I was making up for all those years when any drinking I managed had to be away from the prying eyes of Tam Paton. We also worked on the house. It was a very, very happy time.

Bereft fans did turn up in Dollar during those early months. One girl had travelled hundreds of miles. She had got a cab from Edinburgh and asked the driver to wait outside the pub. She came in and burst into tears. Threw her arms around me and then turned, walked out and got back in her cab. I didn't know how to react in these situations. Sometimes I'd get in from the pub and there would be two or more tartan-clad teenagers sitting in the kitchen. Dad had found them in the grounds and invited them in for coffee.

There were some campaigns and noise from the girls about my leaving. I heard there was a deluge of letters and cards at the fan club but, of course, Tam ensured they never got through to me. It died down quickly and fan visits to Dollar became less frequent. That is what I wanted. Ian Mitchell had built a solid and enthusiastic following in a remarkably fast time. I was quickly out of sight, out of mind.

I kept tabs on what was happening in Rollerworld. In November of 1976 Ian Mitchell left the Rollers citing unbearable pressure; his tenure had lasted just six months. Tam later put him in another group he managed called Rosetta Stone. Ian was replaced by a guy called Pat McGlynn. Pat lasted for less time than even Ian did. He found himself airbrushed off an album cover. Many years later he would reveal what made him quit.

One of the funnier things that happened while I was out of the group was Tam Paton's engagement to Marcella Knaiflova. It was a cynical and shallow attempt to throw the press off the scent of his homosexuality. A better plan would have been him being less reckless in his private life. There were photo shoots and ridiculous statements from Tam about falling head over heels in love. Marcella came out of nowhere and was soon forgotten.

Although *I Only Want to Be with You* had done well there was a sense that Rollermania had cooled down in the UK. However, it had not yet peaked in America and beyond. There were scenes of fan hysteria from the very first concert at Steel Pier in Atlantic City right through to the gigs in Canada in June. One newspaper reported after a concert in front of 9,000 screaming girls in Edmonton:

> When it was all over, when the screaming had faded, the smoke had cleared, and the 27 fainting, hysterical girls had been cared for, it was obvious that something had gone wrong.

The band had to leave the stage twice at the Northlands Coliseum before the promoters came on stage and started unplugging guitars and ending the show prematurely. Girls had been rushing the stage and the lack of control and mass hysteria freaked the Canadians. In Toronto 40,000 fans turned up to see the Rollers play in Nathan Phillips Square. Canada had fallen.

Later in the year the band conquered New Zealand and Japan. Both countries went Roller mad and Japan, particularly, embarked on a love affair with the group that persists strongly to this day. There was even talk of us touring Russia but Russia itself put a stop to that one stating in one newspaper that we would not be invited as we were 'stupefying the minds of the masses'.

Early in 1977, the Rollers recorded the *It's a Game* album. The hugely respected Harry Maslin produced. Harry worked with David Bowie to make the *Young Americans* and *Station to Station* albums earning him iconic status. I think it is one of the best albums by the band, even though (because?) I wasn't on it. The tracks *Don't Let the Music Die*, written by Eric and Stuart and *The Way I Feel Tonight* are two of the Bay City Rollers' best efforts ever. *Don't Let the Music Die* is my all time favourite Rollers number. The latter song was written by Harvey Shield who had once been in a band called Episode Six that also included Roger Glover and Ian Gillan who later joined Deep Purple.

The album was reasonably well received by the critics. Chas de Whalley in *Sounds* even said *It's a Game* was a 'pretty classy pop product':

> Harry Maslin has endowed the Rollers with a depth of sound normally only associated with more 'mature' west coast pop rockers, like the Bellamy Brothers. From a band like the Rollers who have come in for so much stick over the last few years, *It's a Game* really isn't too bad.

You can almost feel the words sticking in Chas's throat.

Commercially, though, *It's a Game* continued the retreat from chart dominance. The album made only 18 in the UK and not even the top 20 in the US. The title single *It's A Game* only hit 16 in the UK. *You Made Me Believe In Magic* did better hitting ten in the US but only 34 in UK. *The Way I Feel Tonight* made 24 in the US. These were disappointing numbers, especially in the UK. The Bay City Rollers were to never have another singles hit in the UK after *You Made Me Believe in Magic*.

In Britain something had happened that had shaken the music scene to its core – punk. A record called *Anarchy in the UK* by the Sex Pistols galvanised a generation and for a short while revolution and saliva was in the air. The band appeared on a live London teatime chat show and told the presenter to fuck off! This was a first in 1976. They had an album with a picture of the Queen with a safety pin through her nose as she celebrated her 25-year jubilee. The punk look kicked out what had gone before and could have been seen as two fingers to the smartly dressed Mod with torn jeans, dirty vests, purple spiky hair and boots. Mind you tartan trousers did survive into the punk era. I always thought Johnny Rotten looked like Woody after he'd been stuck in a tumble-dryer for a couple of hours. The Rollers and many of the glam rock stalwarts were swept aside.

The Pistols led the charge at home, but they are said to have been influenced and triggered even by The Ramones from New York who played a legendary gig at the Roundhouse in Camden in the summer of 1976. Some music historians pinpoint this performance as the birth of punk in Britain. The Ramones song *Blitzkrieg Bop* having been a rallying call for some of the future punk musicians. So even though many believe punk was a nail in the coffin of the Bay City Rollers there is a school of thought that indirectly we were the forefathers of the entire punk movement!

The Ramones themselves have acknowledged the influence of the Bay City Rollers on them. Craig Leon, the Ramones' producer, said:

> The Rollers were high up on the list of bands the Ramones would think were very cool. Two things were very influential – the idea of quick, three-minute pop songs and everyone having a uniform look where the fans copied what the band looked like.

The Ramones copied the football terrace chant-style introduction to the Rollers' US number one single, *Saturday Night* for their signature punk anthem, *Blitzkrieg Bop*.

I don't see how anyone has missed this. The opening of *Saturday Night* is virtually the same as *Blitzkrieg Bop*. If it's not note for note, word for word, it's a direct homage. The Ramones sub-stituted 'Hey! Ho! Let's go!' for the Rollers' 'S-A-T-U-R-D-A-Y night' chant.

Drummer Tommy Ramone has added: 'There was a big hit by the Bay City Rollers at the time called *Saturday Night*, which was a chant-type song. So, I thought it would be fun to do for the Ramones too. And somehow I came up with "Hey! Ho! Let's go!".'

In May of 1977 as the band embarked on their second US tour where they were still deeply immersed in Rollermania despite the decline at home I released a record. It had been a year or so now of my life of bucolic leisure and I was becoming a wee bit restless. I had written some songs during my time with the Rollers and since and wanted to show them to someone. One was about my frustration of not having an outlet for the creativity I felt I had inside me that I was too shy to push forward. It was called *I've Got Songs*.

Bell agreed to record and release it, which thrilled me. But they said, honestly, that they felt that a song by an established song-writer would be safer for a debut solo single. They asked Russ Ballard if he had anything for me.

Russ Ballard was well respected in the industry. He had started out in Adam Faith's backing group the Roulettes. He moved on to Unit 4 Plus 2, who had a memorable mid-1960s hit with *Concrete and Clay*, but Russ really established himself in the band Argent, writing their big hit *God Gave Rock and Roll To You*.

Russ suggested a number called *I'm Confessing* which I really liked. What I didn't know was that he also had in his back pocket at the time *So You Win Again*. It was given to Hot Chocolate and became the ninth bestselling single of the year and all-time classic. I recorded *I'm Confessing* and *I've Got Songs*. I remember Helen Shapiro was in the studio at the same time and we both did a bit of background humming on each other's numbers. Bell put out *I'm Confessing* on the A side and *I've Got Songs* on the flip.

I was told that Bell would put some muscle behind the release with wide-spread advertising and that a *Top of the Pops* appearance was guaranteed on the strength of me being a former Bay City Roller. The *TOTP* slot, as we have already seen, had the power to make or break a song or artist. None of this really happened and the single died a quiet death. I heard it did well in Israel. A quick check on the internet reminds me it made number 44 in Aus-tralia in August 1977. The Rollers with *You Made Me Believe in Magic* just pipped me, making 43 in the same month. I learned later that Tam Paton, despite publicly wishing me luck in my solo career and offering to manage me, had lobbied fiercely against the song and me with Arista and anyone else that mattered. He didn't want an ex-Roller to enjoy a solo career. What sort of message would that send to the others? If they thought there was life after the BCRs they might want to sample it and then bang goes Tam's empire and power. Tam had made threats about moving the Rollers away from Arista should my career get pushed. He boasted about this to someone who later told me. Of course, his main fear was Les getting solo career ideas.

I now understood the depth of Tam Paton's Machiavellian side. He was not on my or our side. He was only on Tam's side.

14

Strangers in the Wind

EARLY IN 1978 I got a call at home from Jake Duncan. Jake was our long-time friend and long-time road manager. He suggested that I might want to fly out to Montreux in Switzerland where the Bay City Rollers were recording their sixth studio album *Strangers in the Wind*.

'What for?' I asked.

'I think they need you to help with this album,' Jake replied.

I wasn't sure what the cryptic message was all about, but Jake was quite insistent. I knew that he would not be inviting me out to the recording sessions without an instruction from the rest of the band, or at least some of them. I also thought it was unlikely they wanted me as a session musician bearing in mind they had access to the cream of the session musician world. Nicky Hopkins, keyboards man and session musician to the likes of The Who, The Rolling Stones and The Kinks worked on *Strangers*. He played organ or piano on some of the most famous classics of all time, including *Revolution* by The Beatles, *Tumbling Dice* by the Rolling Stones and *You Are So Beautiful* by Joe Cocker.

Tam used to call himself the sixth Roller but if anyone was qualified to call himself that it was Jake. He is Edinburgh born and bred and back in 1973 he was working as a trainee manager in a hotel. His friend was looking for a co-driver to pilot us to a gig down in Bournemouth. We needed two drivers on mammoth trips like that. Jake got a taste for life on the road with a pop band and his timing turned out to be good. Jake remained with us for many years on and off and was a stable presence in an increasingly mad world.

His overture came at a good time. I had been out of the band for two years, but I had maintained good relations with all the boys. I was also bored. My craving for the quiet life had been sated. Riding, fishing and drinking was great, but not every day. My solo career was going nowhere and never would while Tam Paton wielded influence, so I boarded a plane to Switzerland.

It turned out that the band was in turmoil. The arguments and differences that were festering when I was in the group had been allowed to surface now the mania had calmed down. There was time to be introspective and analytical; before all these feelings and frustrations bubbled away but because of the relentless schedule there was never the opportunity for them to really boil over. The group were down to four with the departures of Ian Mitchell and Pat McGlynn in quick succession. Tam was less in evidence. Fault lines had opened between Les and Eric. Stuart supported Eric and Derek kept his own counsel gradually withdrawing into himself. Eric wanted the Rollers to become artists that were taken seriously and judged on their own creative work. Les worried about alienating the fans and the commerciality of that Rollers' own material written by Eric and Woody. He believed that following Eric's path would accelerate the decline in popularity that was already apparent. Eric was adamant that not following his path or changing radically was even more dangerous.

Jake and others (possibly, even Tam) believed or hoped that I would become a mediating and stabilising influence on the dynamic and perhaps, for a time, I was. The album was finished and first it was announced that I had played on it and then that I had rejoined the band. There was no big meeting. No negotiation. It was just sort of – you might as well come back. Shrug. Why not? From a financial point of view, I think I naively thought if I can't get my money out of the pot I might as well jump back in and we'll all get it out later. I guess Arista and Tam were thinking about arresting the decline in popularity and felt that getting the 'classic' line-up back together would be a solid building block to doing that.

I have fond memories of Montreux, Switzerland and the album. Woody played bass mostly and I moved around on rhythm guitar and keyboards. I thoroughly enjoyed the freedom and the whole experience. Unfortunately, the public and many of our fans did not feel the same way as when it was released later in the year both the album and the singles taken from it failed to chart on both sides of the Atlantic. Some Rollers fans believe *Strangers* to be our best album. It was certainly, with Harry Maslin at the helm, one of the best crafted. The opening track, *Another Rainy Day in New York City*, written by Eric and Woody, was an atmospheric and moody song but possibly too sudden a break with the Rollers people were used to.

Harry Doherty in *Melody Maker* really didn't like it:

> *Strangers in the Wind* portrays the Bay City Rollers as a tired and spent force, and when placed alongside the creative efforts of youngsters like the Radiators, Rezillos and Flys, this album sounds absolutely pathetic. The album is bland, harmless and totally dispensable slop pop.

Why hold back, Harry? Tell us what you really think.

Our commercial star was fading but there was one final world-exposure, surreal interlude. The Americans gave us our own TV series.

Sid and Marty Krofft were Canadian brothers who had made a fortune from puppet shows on American television. Puppetry ran in the family and the boys and their father had appeared in circuses before breaking into the TV big-time with the *Banana Splits* TV show in 1968. The series was made by Hanna-Barbera, creators of *Huckleberry Hound* and *The Flintstones*, and mixed animation with live-action as it followed the adventures of a bubble gum pop group which was made up of animals with human characteristics. Many of the bands I met over the years were humans with animal characteristics. The catchy theme tune *One Banana, Two Banana, La, La, La, La, La, La* was on the lips of 1960s and 1970s children all over the world for a couple of years, to the annoyance of their parents.

The entrepreneurial and creative brothers then launched *H.R. Pufnstuf*, a series about a ship-wrecked boy being washed up on an island populated by an array of fantasy characters. Pufnstuf the friendly dragon (a descendant of Puff, the magic dragon, perhaps?) and Witchiepoo, an inept witch, were the key Krofft creations. The boy was played by Britain's own Jack Wild who I'd met at that strange party when we first arrived in London. Jack had shot to fame when he played the Artful Dodger in the film *Oliver!* The character he was playing in *H.R. Pufnstuf* was meant to be 12 but poor Jack was nearly 30 by this time. I knew how he felt. The television series was so successful it spawned a feature film of the same name.

The Krofft brothers and their puppets competed with Jim Henson and his Muppets for non-human superstardom in the 1970s. By the time we got involved with the brothers Jim Henson was forging ahead. *The Muppet Show* was winning awards and accolades all over and its leading man and woman – Kermit the Frog and Miss Piggy – were almost as popular as Elizabeth Taylor and Richard Burton.

In the spring of 1978 we were offered a series on NBC, the oldest and biggest US TV network at the time. The latest show from the brothers was called *The Krofft Superstar Hour* and was a loose showcase for Krofft characters past and present. We were to be a real life band in comedy sketches shared with H.R. Pufnstuf, Witchiepoo and the gang.

I thought it was a terrific opportunity and the fact that a leading television network in the States wanted to do a show based around us was a big vote of confidence. I also had fond memories of making *Shang-A-Lang*, the TV series, and believe it did us no harm at all. But, the others had mixed feelings. In the case of Les they weren't even mixed – he thought it was a terrible idea and that we'd become a laughing stock. The lure of a couple of months living in Hollywood while the series was made was too strong, even for Les, and we went for it.

That summer of 1978, although seen by some observers as the death throes of the Bay City Rollers, was a marvellous time for me and I remember it with great affection. It was the summer when the hopes of the Scottish nation were pinned on our national football team going to Argentina to compete in the World Cup. England hadn't even qualified and some 'experts' were even saying that Scotland could win it. We didn't. But, before we were dumped out at the group stage, Archie Gemmill scored *that* goal.

Around this time, I was lucky enough to squeeze a holiday in with Dad. He missed Mum terribly, although he tried not to show it. I took him to Torremolinos and it was the first time he'd been abroad outside of military service. He loved every minute. British Airways managed to lose his case which meant he had no clothes and they kindly gave him the cash to go out and buy some new ones. He enjoyed this immensely and even more so when his case turned up and the airline didn't seem too fussed about him giving the newly purchased clothes back. Every morning he'd tap on my door at 7am. Bleary-eyed I'd answer it and Dad was standing there upright and fresh in smart new clothes.

'And what's on the agenda today, son?'

In the wider world our acquaintances The Bee Gees were atop of the world and I, for one, was thrilled for them as I remembered our chat all those years ago when things were not looking so great for them. They'd written the music for *Saturday Night Fever* the film that was breaking box office records across the world and had now followed it up with *Grease*. Disco as a musical genre had been unleashed on the world. The great and good were queuing up at Barry Gibb's door begging for a song. It was a heady time.

John Travolta and Olivia Newton-John were everywhere, and we were in the epicentre while all that was going on. We attended the premiere of *Grease* in America where I chatted with Olivia. We'd met before on *Top of the Pops* and she was, as then, a modest, sweet girl. My mind went back to that *TOTP* recording. Olivia walked past me and gave me a lovely smile and said 'Hello'. I smiled back but looked down at the floor to hide my blushes. Practically ran back to the dressing room and closed the door behind me, leaning up against it as if Olivia would be following me and shoulder barging the door.

'I just saw Olivia Newton-John.'

'What happened?'

'She smiled.'

The boys gathered around me.

'And?'

'That was it…'

Their interest piqued and then deflated they just returned huffily to what they were doing.

Olivia deserved the adulation she was receiving. Anyone who was any-one was at this premiere and even though I was part of a pop phenomenon myself I remained star-struck in the presence of all these celluloid faces.

We rented houses in Los Angeles. Everyone was famous. Dean Martin's son Craig worked on the show and through him I went to see his Dad in his show at the MGM Hotel in Las Vegas. He came to our table and introduced himself. I was with my girlfriend. The Paton nonsense over not having girl-friends was dead in the water now. Dean was clutching a glass of apple juice. His son said that contrary to his reputation his father did not drink alcohol. Later, when I went to settle my bill the waiter said that Dean Martin had kindly paid it. I nodded over to him and thanked him and got up to leave the table and my waiter returned and smiled graciously.

'Mr Martin has paid your tab, Sir, but he has not paid your tip.'

They take their gratuities seriously in California.

California dreaming. We'd all had houses rented for us and cars sup-plied. I asked for a truck. My house was in Laurel Canyon. Les had seen a house that Elton John had lived in. I want one like that, he said. You can have one like that, said the realtor but it costs about ten times the others. Les realised that may be pushing it. Eric and Woody took an apartment that was owned by Stevie Wonder. It was like living on one big film set. Go to the drive-through for a burger and milk shake and you'd see someone and think I know him or her and then you realised you recognised them from the telly. Les got friendly with Britt Ekland. She'd just come out of a relationship with Rod Stewart. He'd been so infatuated he'd written *You're In My Heart* about her. I could see why. I remember having lunch at her place one day and she got up to answer her door. She came back and sat down shaking her head.

'That was Ryan O'Neal,' she said. 'I told him to go away, I'm with the Bay City Rollers.'

Life had become surreal. One evening I drank at the bar of the Beverly Hills Hotel with Barbra Streisand and Robert Redford. I was now drinking a lot, but it was at the stage where I didn't perceive that as a bad thing. Excessive drinking as a young man is a leisure pursuit, excessive drinking in middle age is a hard-to-break habit and excessive drinking in old age is rare. Big drinkers are lucky to make it there. I sought out parties and my Roller status ensured easy entrance. Here I ran into Keith Moon and got pissed with him a couple of times. I also bumped into Sid Vicious of The Sex Pistols but swerved meeting him because he seemed like a bit of dickhead to me. We were also socialising with stars that were guests on the show: Erik Estrada from *Chips*, Scott Baio from *Happy Days* and Joe Namath, the American footballer among them.

One night I was in the Beverly Wilshire Hotel. I'd been booked to appear on a chat show in New York. A car and a plane had been arranged and I was advised to get some sleep as my escort would be fetching me in a few hours. I retired to my room. I easily went off to sleep but was rudely awakened not long after by a loud banging on the left-hand adjoining door. Dragged myself out of bed and opened it. There stood Keith Moon in tee-shirt and underpants, grinning from ear to ear, holding a bottle of champagne in each hand. I couldn't help but notice that attached to each arm was a smiling, naked girl.

'It's party time, old Roller,' he said and stepped into my room.

'No, Keith. It's not party time for me. I have to be in New York soon. I need to get some sleep,' I replied as I gently ushered him back over his threshold. Moon looked at me as if it were me that was mad. Perhaps, I was.

Later in the night I was awoken again. This time it was tapping on the right-hand adjoining door. It happened three or four times, but I ignored it assuming it was The Who drummer again trying to trick me or someone worse (John Bonham, perhaps) trying to entice me into their web.

My chauffeur cum minder duly came and fetched me and as I passed reception I asked the guy behind the desk who was in the room next door to me.

'We're dreadfully sorry, that was Keith Moon. We do apologise for the noise.'

'No, no, the other side of me.'

The concierge consulted a book on the desk.

'On the other side Mr Longmuir that is, let me check now... Olivia Newton John.'

I don't know if it was Olivia that was tapping that night. It could have been her maid. Who knows? But, I like to think so. Que sera sera.

It was a shock and terribly sad when Keith Moon died just weeks later at the same London flat where Mama Cass had also expired a few years before when she choked on her own vomit. He was a young London lad showered with money, glory and adulation at a very early age. He obviously didn't have a Tam Paton type to keep him in order and he went for it. It's a shame because if he had lasted another couple of years he'd have calmed down and would be a national treasure now appearing on chat shows reminiscing about the mad nights out with Jimi Hendrix. Someone must die, I guess, for the survivors to talk about.

I had my 30th birthday party in Hollywood. Not bad for a laddie from Dalry with his pockets hanging out his trousers. My girlfriend Julie was with me along with a host of stars and regulars on the Hollywood party scene. I woke up bruised in the morning from pinching myself. Another time Julie and I were eating quietly in a small restaurant. A middle-aged couple entered and sat down behind Julie.

'Promise me you won't look round?'

'I won't look round.'

'Paul Newman is sitting behind you.'

Julie let out a little yelp and promptly spun around. Paul Newman smiled graciously. I guess it happened all the time. I knew his eyes were blue but to see them in real life was hypnotising. He would have had no idea who I was.

Me being out with Julie was now not an issue. The old Rollers 'rules' no longer held fast. I had Julie with me in America, but all the boys were now free and some formed relationships and openly pursued women. Especially, Les. For the first time we were off the leash when we were in America. Paton had dropped all the milk-drinking nonsense and was rarely with us. The façade with his 'fiancé' had been dropped and his homosexuality now an open secret. From all accounts (including his own) he was gallivanting around the globe enjoying his wealth, popping his pills and chasing young men. We just had no idea then how young they were. The job of looking after us and running the business side of things fell to poor old Jake Duncan.

A taster show went out on NBC on 8 September 1978 and we sang *Saturday Night*, *Money Honey*, *I Only Want to Be with You* and *Rock and Roll Love Letter*. I thought it came across okay, bearing in mind it was primarily aimed at children. The critics begged to differ. Well, they didn't even beg. They hated it. The Scottish accents appeared to be a problem and we were compared unfavourably to The Monkees.

Nevertheless, the series proper broadcast the next day, Saturday morning, under the title *The Krofft Superstar Hour* and the reception and viewing figures did not meet expectations. The network maybe didn't see us as the problem because after eight episodes they renamed it *The Bay City Rollers Show* and cut the running time from one hour to 30 minutes. The last episode went out in January 1979 and no more were commissioned. That was the end of that. It was fun while it lasted. I loved the show, to be honest. I guess I believed that we as a group or individuals needed to acquire new skills to develop and acting seemed to me a route worth exploring.

Before the plug was pulled Les McKeown left the Bay City Rollers. With hindsight I now see that as the end of the Bay City Rollers 'classic' version. His anger at having to do the TV show that he believed was demeaning boiled over. Les was right it was demeaning in many ways. But, that is with hindsight. It could have been good. It could have achieved some sort of cult status and we were not exactly spoilt for choice at the time. He was surly and uncooperative while shooting in rehearsals and he didn't take kindly to having an unscripted custard pie pushed in his face in one episode. That was Marty Krofft's idea.

One time Marty sought me out.

'What's the matter with that bum? He's so far up his own arse you can see daylight. I'll end up tearing his head off. Can you sing, Alan?' Marty went on to say he wanted to fire Les there and then if I would agree to take on the singing.

'I can sing, Marty but I'll not go on for Les,' I replied.

I had not been back in the band long and those feelings of warm reunion that were so strong in Switzerland had receded fast and the amnesty had been broken. The band was surly and aggressive with one another. I hated all the negativity and could feel my earlier despair returning. I just kept a lid on it.

The point of no return, though, was reached in Japan where we toured immediately after filming had stopped for the Krofft series. I had long given up being the peacemaker. There was no peace to be had.

We were on the slide in the UK, going off the boil in the US, but in Japan Rollermania was just hitting peak fervour. The girls didn't go so mad like at home, but the intensity of their adoration transmitted from them to us as they craned their necks and stared maniacally was tangible. You felt the audiences in Japan were like time-bombs waiting to explode. We played the Budokan, Tokyo's premier music venue with a capacity of 15,000 three nights in a row. Les was behaving erratically, or should I say normally by now, he went crowd surfing a couple of times which alarmed our security and enraged the local police. It wasn't in the plan. In the dressing room someone threw a can at Les and it hit him. Fisticuffs before a gig is never a good thing. We were playing in Shizuoka and Les got annoyed whenever the spotlight moved away from him. He moved in on Woody's guitar solo and nudged him aside. Woody didn't see the joke and lined up a kick, booting Les clean off the stage. Les clambered back up and waded into Woody. A scrum ensued. I stood there motionless strumming my guitar.

'This is it. This is it,' I thought.

15
Yesterday's Heroes

AND THAT WAS it, in my mind, at least. The end of the main event. The Bay City Rollers limped on but by the close of 1978 the glory days were over. From *Keep on Dancing* to Les quitting had been seven long years. From *Remember* to now had been only four frantic years. In one way it went quickly in other ways those four years could have been 40.

We desperately tried to recalibrate and to reinvent ourselves. We changed our name to The Rollers and released the album *Elevator*. Duncan Faure, the lead singer with a successful South African band called Rabbit, had replaced Les as lead singer. I saw history repeat itself as the fans cried 'we want Les' as he tried to perform in the early gigs. It was Eric's idea to drop the Bay City but we all agreed. To stand a chance in the coming decade we had to change. The teenybopper image had to go. If nothing else because we weren't teeny-boppers anymore. I was now an elderly man in my 30s. I'm not sure of my exact age, only Tam could tell us that.

Elevator contained songs written by all of us and we were generally very proud of it. It was our attempt to catch the new wave. We recorded it at DublinSound and a guy called Peter Ker produced. Peter's main claim to fame was that he had co-written the number one 1960s hit *Fire!* recorded by the Crazy World of Arthur Brown. That was another iconic *Top of the Pops* appearance. Old Arthur prancing around the stage wearing a hat fully alight. BBC Health and Safety would be running around after him with fire extinguishers these days. The problem with the album was unlike a real elevator it didn't even go up the charts to be able to come down again.

Eric was the main member pushing for the evolution into an altogether edgier outfit. Some writers have marked this as the cause of our downfall, but this isn't fair or accurate. We could not have gone on as the Bay City Rollers pumping out *Bye Bye Baby* soundalikes and continued with some high-profile momentum. Our down was already falling. The world had changed, the music had changed, and we had changed. It was the right decision, but it was not enough. It was too late. Like Les and Nobby before him Duncan was a good singer, a talented musician and not lacking in charisma but it was still too late to arrest the decline. Sure, we could still earn money (for others) and there remained a smaller, committed fan-base but the glory years with the classic line-up were over. Except in Japan, where they continued to lap us up.

In 1979 we toured Germany. Of all the mainland European countries the Germans seemed to appreciate us the most. It was a short tour, but Tam hadn't even bothered to attend. He'd sent some young 21-year-old kid to manage things. Nothing against the boy but he was too young for anybody to take seriously and security in the venues was not being taken care of. One venue was a 12,000-seater. That's a big gig to be managed by a young, inexperienced laddie. We were fuming about this and we decided it was time to sack Tam Paton. Woody and I phoned him up and I did the talking.

Tam and I had been through a lot together and although it is tempting to allow what happened after to colour what went before I still thought then he was a good man that went bad. The Rollers wouldn't have happened without him and his talent, drive and loyalty in those early years cannot be challenged. However, now in 1979, it was clear he'd lost interest. It was becoming clear too he'd lost the plot too. He was going rotten. It was not a hard decision to pick up the telephone and sack him. After all, it was my band. I started the Bay City Rollers and I hired Tam. It was my responsibility.

I opened by moaning about the Germany experience. Tam just listened. He didn't offer up a defence.

'Anyway, Tam, we've decided to sack you.'

'That's fine, Alan. Just fine. Guid luck.'

He didn't seem bothered. I don't think he was either. He was probably relieved. The juggernaut had left him behind too. Tam was out of his depth with the big shots in London and New York and he knew he couldn't solve the missing money problem. He'd been had too although unlike us he had been able to feather his nest in those early years before the white-collared hordes started slurping from the pot.

Now we had time to think and examine our careers – where we had been and where we were going – we found some common ground again. We all wanted to know where our money was. Even Les was united with us on that one. We weren't starving by any means and hadn't been since before *Keep on Dancing* and we'd all availed ourselves of houses and cars and wanted for nothing on a day-to-day basis but even us naïve lads knew that the money that had passed through our hands was a tiny fraction of the many millions that had been generated. Nobody could give us answers that offered us any comfort.

As early as 1979 I heard about one of our 'advisers' boasting that his large house in one of North London's most prestigious roads was paid for courtesy of the Bay City Rollers. I will not name him because he may be still alive and if he sues me I do not have the money to defend myself. The reason I do not have the money to defend myself is because this man (and many, many others) have it. Imagine that, someone suing you for what money you have left with the money you should have had. You couldn't make it up.

The intricacies of the money trail and the associated legal actions have been covered in detail elsewhere. I will not attempt to catalogue it here but suffice to say that the legal cases kicked off in 1979 and only concluded fully in 2017. Therefore, they lasted 38 years, on and off, over three times as long as the Bay City Rollers proper did themselves. Madness. By the end of it the professional advisers in whose interests it was to keep the action going had swam around in our pot and snorted almost every penny and dime up their cavernous nostrils.

I got to know lawyers and their offices well. It always amazed me how they presented smartly in their pin-stripes, braces and ties yet their offices were often musty and untidy with volumes of books and unanswered mail strewn across desks, chairs and the floor. Ashtrays overflowing. Miraculously, when needing to check a point of law, they could wade into the disorder and pluck a reference book from the piles and quote from it.

In New York, in the offices of one firm, I was sitting opposite one young, thrusting lawyer. It was all very Michael Douglas in *Wall Street*. We were discussing something I had apparently agreed to. I never agreed to this thing, whatever it was, it was never discussed with me.

'The problem is Mr Longmuir, you've actually signed a document to this effect.'

My mind went back to the countless times Tam Paton and others shoved documents under our noses to sign just before we were to go on stage.

'Show me.'

The lawyer pushed the document across the desk. The scrawl was not recognisable as my signature. It was not recognisable as anyone's signature. This was what we were up against. The contempt for us, from the people supposedly working for us, was so high they didn't even present us with the documents they just forged our signatures.

I sometimes wondered as the most mature band member (in my mid-20s) whether I should have been more alert to the business pitfalls that opened around us so quickly. In an ideal world I should have been. But I was still very young myself, a plumber by training and trusting by nature.

In 1979 we went to South Africa. Duncan was still a big draw there and now he was part of the Bay City Rollers it made us a compelling proposition. Tour dates were scheduled, and we were playing 5,000 plus venues. We were big news and were approached by Barrie St Clair about making a film. Barrie was a film producer who had just enjoyed some success in helping bring out the film *Zulu Dawn*. It was essentially a prequel to the legendary *Zulu* film. The film is generally considered inferior to the first one that made Michael Caine super famous but nevertheless attracted the likes of Peter O'Toole, Burt Lancaster and John Mills to the cast.

Barrie wanted to cash in on our draining popularity and proposed using us in a film called *Burning Rubber* which was a story based around drag racing and about a geeky car mechanic who becomes a top drag racer and ends up winning the affections of the out-of-his-league female co-star, the very beautiful Olivia Pascal. I was gobsmacked when I was offered the male lead, one Henry Carstens. It was one of those moments when you looked behind you to see if there is someone else there they are offering the part to. Of course, I accepted. Could this be a way out from the Rollers? Filming began in 1980.

The film, to be honest, has not stood the test of time. I'm not sure it stood the test of anything much. I was given a haircut and glasses that made me look like John Denver. No offence, John. The rest of the band played themselves as my fellow mechanics and band members. I did my best, but the reviews were generally poor, and it didn't do good box office, as they say. But, again, I enjoyed it. I had no experience as an actor so going from skits in *Shang-A-Lang* and *Superstars* to leading man was a serious jump. Bearing that in mind I didn't think I was disastrous and would have got better had there been further opportunities. Unfortunately, and understandably, there wasn't.

But, I got to star in a film. Star in a film. Let that sink in, Alan. I'm just a plumber from Edinburgh. I got to snog Olivia Pascal. Google her. She was (and I'm sure she still is) stunningly beautiful. I learned a bit about camera craft. I observed at first-hand how films were made and how important things like continuity were. It was a great learning experience. The director was an Irishman named Norman Cohen. I'm not sure what he was doing in South Africa as he had been director on the film adaptions of TV's *Till Death Us Do Part* and *Dad's Army* and had just come off the run of *Confessions* sex comedy films that may not be considered high art these days, but they sure took the money at the gate.

We were soon back to reality. Back in America. We'd finally left Arista, who we were now in dispute with over unpaid royalties, and had signed a deal with

Epic Records. We did manage to make an album *Ricochet* amid the chaos and crumbling but it did not make any commercial impact. In 1981 Duncan Faure, fed up and annoyed about not seeing any real money (the rest of us were accustomed to it), went back to South Africa. We did get some money out of the mire around this time, but it barely covered the huge tax bills that were now landing on our mats. Tax due on the earnings we had not seen.

Derek was thoroughly disillusioned with the whole thing. Being a pop star was not for him anymore. In 1984 he quietly quit the band, never to return. A few years later he trained as a nurse. Although us brothers had started the band and craved success and adulation it never sat comfortably with us. We were not genetically wired up to bask in the public eye. We preferred to stand back and let others absorb the flashlights and attention. Perhaps it was the undertaker in us.

I retreated to Dollar to lick my wounds. To come to terms with the end of my old band. I had mixed feelings about it all. I found solace in the Dollar Arms.

One day I was at home in Dollar and I could see a small Citroën car parked up in the distance. I wandered out to take a closer look. There was a very pretty young girl sitting in the driving seat who seemed terrified by my approach. I tapped on the window.

'You don't remember me, do you?' she smiled, nervously.

There was a flicker of recognition on my part.

'Angela from Bermuda. Remember? I won the competition and me and my Mum holidayed with you.'

Of course, I remembered. It was the Gales Honey competition and Angela had been the fan who got to spend some time with all of us when we had a few recovery days in Bermuda back in 1975. Last time I saw her we were skidding around on mopeds in the Bermudan sunshine. Her name was Angela and she had since studied at Liverpool University. She had bloomed into a beautiful young woman. She had driven up from Wetherby in Yorkshire. I was touched by her determination and invited her inside. I liked her personality and we got on very well and arranged to see each other again. She cooked a great meal. She took me mountain climbing. I was smitten, and it was a great feeling. Angela and I ended up having a two-year relationship which eventually did not survive the geographical distance between us and my long periods away from home but for a while we were very happy and close.

Some years later I was playing a Butlins with one of the 1990s incarnations of the group and I noticed a woman looking up at me. Her hair was different, but it was Angela. She smiled, and I smiled. We had a lovely chat afterwards and Angela told me she was happily married with children. Our relationship never ended in acrimony, it just fizzled. I was happy she was happy.

My relationship with Angela was a welcome respite from the mess that the Rollers had become. At one point Ian Mitchell and Pat McGlynn re-joined the band for a brief period and we were a seven-piece. We played gigs in Japan and elsewhere and some were very well attended but there was no continuity to our careers and the only interest the media showed in us was to pick over the bones of what they liked to report as our messy demise.

In 1982, the media had a valid reason to report negatively. Tam Paton was arrested, charged, tried and sentenced to three years in prison for having sex with underage boys. It came as a shock to me. Tam served one year inside for these offences although he never really accepted them or showed any remorse. He was happy to go on television and in print to claim that his crimes would not have been so if they were committed across the border in England where the age of consent was 16. He presented himself as a gay man persecuted by archaic Scottish law and prejudice. I do not know the detail of the offences nor do I wish to, but I have read one of the boys was only 15, which somewhat negates his stance. I saw an interview where Tam was trying to deflect matters by banging on about one of his victims being the youngest soldier to serve in the Falkland Islands conflict.

The last time I saw Tam face to face was when I visited him at his fortress, Little Kellerstain, which lurked furtively off the airport road. The site is nowadays hidden by the headquarters of the Royal Bank of Scotland. Perhaps Tam chose the location so when he retired he could spend more time with his money. Sorry, our money. It was a ranch-like building that Tam had built to his own specifications in the 1970s – and it showed. From the outside you could be looking at a small town doctors' surgery and on the inside it was pine-panelled like a Swedish sauna. I expected to open a door and find ABBA sitting in a room on space hoppers eating Curly Wurlys. There was a row of identically kitted out bedrooms which altered the mood and aroused suspicion. There was also a sauna and plunge pool inside and a swimming pool outside. It must have been the only property in Edinburgh with an outdoor pool, the weather in this part of the world not being conducive to such accoutrements.

This was a good few years before he died, and Tam Paton had become a sight to behold. I knew he was steadily adding weight as the years rolled by but now he was a grey-haired, haunted-looking man weighing near 30 stone. He reminded me of Cyril Smith, the elephantine MP who would later be accused of all sorts of child abuse. He flopped in a chair, legs wide apart, wearing elasticated jogging bottoms and an old, stained shirt. Remote controls were stacked up beside him. He told me proudly he had a control room where there were banks of CCTV screens giving him viewing access to every corner of the house. And there were a lot of corners. I didn't know whether the surveillance was for security or voyeuristic reasons. Both, probably.

I had come to see him to borrow money. Five hundred pounds, I think it was. I was temporarily embarrassed for ready cash and there was a pressing bill to pay. I figured that Tam would be sufficiently guilt-ridden knowing that I knew he knew we'd been royally turned over and because of that he'd lend it to me. I don't recall having any urgent plans to pay it back. I was owed. Before I got to the point I could not help noticing boys drifting around the house. They could have been 14. They could have been 18. Whatever, I don't reckon shaving foam was a major item on the Little Kellerstain shopping list.

'Who are all these boys, Tam?' I asked.

'They're Edinburgh's waifs and strays.'

My brow furrowed.

'Alan, the police bring them here. It's all above board. The police find them on the streets and to keep them out of trouble they bring them here. They know I will give them food and shelter. They know I will put them on the straight and narrow. If they go into care they run away. If they come here, they stay. They get jobs. They go straight.'

Tam could see I was still sceptical.

'Look, Alan. Look at these,' he brandished a bunch of brown envelopes and waved them in front of me. 'Do you know what they are?'

'No.'

'They're Giros. Social Security cheques. I look after these and I look after them. Everyone's happy.'

He smiled his 'aren't I a shrewd businessman' smile and nodded, his chins wobbling with self-satisfaction. I thought this would be a good time to strike.

'I need some money, Tam. I was wondering if you could lend me £1,000?' I was preparing for him to knock me down.

'A grand? I don't have that sort of money, Alan.'

'Five hundred, Tam. I'm really in a tight spot. Only for a few weeks.'

'Och, Alan. As I said, I don't have that type of money.'

I shrugged and smiled. Got up and left. Knowing that one way or another we'd never see each other again.

Tam Paton casts a malevolent shadow over this book. I wanted to keep him out of it, but it has proved impossible. I hope I have kept the bastard at bay, at least. I am sure that more will come out on Tam and that his depravity ran deeper than we currently know. When people ask me for my opinion on him I often say he was a good man, gone bad. As the years have gone by I have gradually begun to realise how bad he had gone. I have been truthful about his physical relationship with me. There was none.

I will not comment on what may or may not have happened with other members of the band other than that if anything of a sexually predatory nature took place I did not know about it at the time and such things were never discussed in my presence. However, how hurtful it would be for me to doubt some terrible experience one of the others had if it had happened and how wrong it would be for me to say it had happened to someone when it hadn't? I really hope not. It's not my business to comment for the others. This is my story. I'm sure if the others wish to tell their story, they will.

Around the time I left the group in 1976, I think I was the first band member to warn the others that Tam was going dodgy. I was talking about him not acting in our best interests not his private life. At the time the others were dismissive. They still trusted and, dare I say it, loved him. We all did at one time. We all knew by 1976 he was gay. We knew his boyfriend Ray. And, yes, his nickname was Gay Ray. I had no inkling until he was convicted that his preference was really young boys and only then did an unwelcome truth start to sink in. Later, I think the drugs destroyed and eroded any moral barriers he had.

In the mid-1980s the lack of money meant I had no choice but to go plumbing again. It really didn't bother me. Newspapers got very excited about the fact that less than ten years after *Bye Bye Baby* swept the world I was rolling my sleeve up and shoving my arm down toilets. But I was not proud. I needed to put food on the table and this was the way I knew. I was self-employed so could take time away when a gig or a small tour came up. For example, in the late 1980s and 1990s I did a lot of gigs with an Eric Faulkner led version of the band. I enjoyed that. I just liked playing and didn't really fret over whose name was in front of the band's or mine.

Back on the road again with Eric's version of The Rollers was a pleasant experience. I was amazed to discover just how many artists from the 1960s and 1970s were still on the road. We played the Butlins circuit and the clubs but between us we packed out the old ballrooms and it was great. There were still some old original Teds left, lots of Mods, Skinheads and Rockers around all mixed up with Rollers fans, now, incredibly, in their 30s plus. All of them dancing together lapping up the nostalgia and the alcohol. If drugs were around they were probably statins.

A few of the bands maintained the original names with no original members which was disconcerting, but most contained at least one or two original faces. From the 1960s there were The Searchers, The Swinging Blue Jeans, Billy J Kramer, Herman's Hermits (minus Herman) and scores of others. From the 1970s: Sweet, Mud, Showaddywaddy, The Glitter Band, Suzi Quatro, Smokie and so on. Punters were getting their money's worth. Time had levelled us all out. There were few egos to deal with. We were all getting paid this time around, which was refreshing. We shared buses together and recounted all the old stories. Some of us liked a drink. Les Gray from Mud and Brian Connolly from Sweet were particularly enthusiastic imbibers.

Standing at the bar at Butlins in Bognor Regis once Les Gray pushed through the throng. Clocked me and Woody at the bar and gave us both a big handshake and backslap.

'Three pints of lager, please, mate,' he called to the barman above the din.

I looked at Woody and smiled and nodded. I was saying good old Les he's buying us a pint. Les turned around the pint jugs very adeptly held between his ringed fingers and nodded again as he weaved his way through the crowd. The three pints were for Les.

My mate Bruce Crawford and I started up a plumbing and heating business and we did alright. Sometimes people recognised me when I turned up with my tools to fix their pipes.

'What are you doing?' they'd ask, incredulous.

'What do you think I'm doing,' I'd reply and get stuck into the work in hand.

I remember one day visiting a posh house in Edinburgh. I had a young apprentice with me who delighted in exposing me to customers. I'd get very embarrassed and tell him to shut up. This day a very well-to-do lady led us both to her kitchen and I quickly crawled underneath the basin area. I heard the boy start.

'You know who that is under there, don't you?'

'No, I can't say I do.'

'He's Alan Longmuir.'

I'm guessing her expression is a bit vague here.

'Alan Longmuir. One of the Bay City Rollers,' says the boy.

I pulled myself into view from under the basin as I needed to locate a spanner. The house-owner stood there arms folded. She looked me up and down and said: 'Yes, and I'm one of The Supremes.'

16

Back on the Street

IN THE MID-1980s I was jogging along splitting my time between plumbing, gigging and touring with various incarnations of the Rollers in smaller and smaller venues and socialising in Dollar. Interest in the band had waned and when we did figure nationally anywhere it was normally to poke fun. Society's shame over wearing tank tops, flared trousers and stack shoes during the 1970s was being heaped upon us. It was as if all the sartorial and cultural cock-ups of the decade were personified and encapsulated by the Bay City Rollers.

I watched Les guest on *The Jonathan Ross Show* one Saturday night. I didn't even know who Ross was. He seemed very young to me to be interviewing big stars many years older than him, but he had a slick look and a quick mind and tongue. People seemed to like him. But he took the rise out of Les and us. The tartan clothes, the twee songs, the bog-brush haircuts. He wanted to rub Les's face in the Rollers' downfall. He had gotten Les on as a vehicle for 15 minutes of piss-taking. I know Les and I could see in his eyes and body language that he wanted to lean forward and lay the head on the schoolboy cockney pipsqueak, but he had an album or show to promote.

Eric didn't help our credibility when he made an advert for Skol lager where he promised the Bay City Rollers would not make a comeback if someone bought him a drink. Funny, I guess, but a bit demeaning for us.

Back in Dollar the landlady of the Dollar Arms invited me to a licensed trade dance and I went along in my kilt and took my Dad. I chatted up a local girl called Jan and we got on very well. I left with her number. We fell in love, courted and eventually married in 1985. It was all very fast, our only child, my son, Jordan James, was born in 1986.

We bought the Castle Campbell Hotel in Dollar full of hope of a long and fulfilling future as hoteliers and publicans. It had eight bedrooms and had seen better and busier days. It started well. We got some newspaper publicity – 'Roller Prefers Pulling Pints' – that sort of thing. Woody's parents kindly came down to wish us well and my celebrity attracted a good early custom. But, soon the reality of running a hospitality business began to bear down on us and our relationship. It was bloody arduous work. My drinking increased, and it was like a vicious circle. The more stressed I became the more whisky I consumed. The more whisky I consumed the less likely I would be to overcome the inherent problems of the business. Things like finding and keeping chefs was a brain ache. Keeping tabs on some dishonest staff in a cash business almost impossible.

The village of Dollar had once been a mining community with plenty of local men with money in their pockets and a raging thirst when their shifts finished, but by the time I came along the last of the collieries had been shut down for a decade. Dollar was a lovely place to live but there were not many dollars to be earnt from the local community. We relied on tourists but that was patchy. The financial and workload pressures increased each year. I had sold my beloved house in the village and borrowed from the brewery to finance the hotel. I was watching my limited assets gush down the plug hole.

Our marriage was breaking down and the final straw came when Jan and I arrived back from a night out and we came in to find the waiters and bar staff strewn around the bar drinking the losses. Jan went mad. She ordered the staff to bed or home and demanded I do something about it.

'In the morning,' I said. I was half-cut and wanted my bed, not a confrontation. But a confrontation was what I got. The police were called, and I was arrested. It is a sorry episode in my life and I so wish it had never happened. If drink wasn't present it would not have. I would have walked away. The papers got hold of it and I winced at the sorry headline 'Bay City Basher'.

The headlines were not factually true, 'Bay City Roller Bashed' would have been more accurate. It a very dark and unhappy time for me. The fact is Jan and I weren't compatible, the relationship wasn't destined to last. The only saving grace was that we produced a beautiful baby boy.

Jan left, taking Jordan with her. The marriage ended that horrible night. It was acrimonious and sadly I did not build the good relationship with my son Jordan that I should have. I hope, one day, I can right those wrongs.

I was left in that hotel where the problems had, unfortunately, not followed my wife out of the door. I had neither the ability or will to carry on. I suffered a mild heart attack. I shut up shop. My creditors queued up outside the pub. The Sheriff's Office became involved. We held an open sale where the fixtures, fittings and assorted crap was sold off to the public. Some turned up just to see the latest humiliation of a Bay City Roller.

Around this time not only was the legal search for our money winding its way through the courts we started suing each other. In hindsight a stupid thing to do when none of us had any money. Les was using the Bay City Rollers name when, of course, it was the Bay City Roller and some other musicians. Eric was incensed and said we should fight it in court. I had no wish to use the Bay City Rollers name for myself so I'm not too sure why I was party to the row. Going with the flow. Keeping the peace as usual. This one limped through the courts, too, ending when a judge ruled that Les could use the name if he prefixed it with something. Les was happy, I think. His band was called Les McKeown's Legendary Bay City Rollers. I suppose we could all have done that, but I suspect if I went out as Alan Longmuir's Original Bay City Rollers I'd have found four or five writs on my doorstep in the morning.

I was rootless now. I stayed in friends' rooms. Today they call it sofa surfing which puts a jocular spin on what is a miserable and humiliating existence. I eventually settled in a flat above the Dollar Arms, which was not ideal, and you don't have to imagine too hard where most of my time was spent. I think that was 1989. I didn't own a bean. I was drinking heavily. I had been celibate for a couple of years, such was my fear of entering a relationship. My dear dad died on 1 February 1989. He had suffered but managed with vascular dementia for some time but oesophageal cancer finally took him. A painful time for my brother and sisters and wider family. I felt even more sorry for myself. I was 40 years old and an orphan. It was my lowest ebb and I feel sad now thinking about it. It makes me want to cry, almost 30 years later.

The absolute nadir, though, was when I lost the flat at the pub and had nowhere to go so for a few days I kipped down in one of the pub's outhouses. Only now, as I recall this, do I realise I was not only homeless but sleeping rough. Lucky the papers never found out. They would have loved it. I can imagine the headlines now: 'Roller Ruined' or 'Down and Out in Dollar' or, best still, 'Keep on Dossing'.

After a few days my friend Chris Balanowski heard where I was sleeping and came and fetched me.

'You'll not be staying here, Alan Longmuir,' he said, and he took me into he and his wife's home, affording me his daughter's bedroom for a few months which gave me a valuable family environment to try and build myself up again. I am forever grateful to Chris who has been a loyal friend to me since we first chanced on each other in a city pub in the 1970s. I was a Roller, he was a budding footballer. We had many adventures together over the years. Chris is one of life's gems.

I can remember being in that outhouse and looking over at my sole possessions: a black bag with a few clothes and toiletries and a guitar. If someone looked at me they'd think I was a tramp. If I'd told them I'd appeared in front of millions of people on *The Ann-Margret Show* and quaffed champagne at the celebrity premier of *Grease* with Olivia Newton-John they'd have laughed. I thought about how, in a pub somewhere, someone was putting one of my records on the juke box. Nobody would have believed it. I don't think I really did.

17

We *Can* Make Music

FORTUNATELY, I WAS down but not quite out. In 1994, I met Eileen Rankin. She was on a hen night and I was attracted to her immediately. She had come back with her friends to the flat of the friend whose house I was minding. I got her number and things went from there. Eileen was a down-to-earth civil servant who was not at all fazed by my celebrity (or former celebrity). She told me she had been a David Cassidy fan anyway when she was a girl. I told her that David had terrible skin – I was jealous at 46 years of age! We courted and finally married in 1998. I was in love and happy again, living with Eileen and her two young sons, Nik and Kyle, from a previous relationship.

I don't just believe, I know, that if I hadn't met Eileen when I did I'd not be here now. I was drinking myself into a premature grave, had lost self-confidence and self-esteem and had not a penny to my name. My depression was never too far from the surface. The positive things that started to happen to me again can be traced back to the time I entered into a relationship with Eileen. It can't be a coincidence.

The years of living in hotels, fractured sleep patterns, bad diet, stress and drinking had taken its toll on my health. In 1995, I had a heart attack which wasn't life-threatening but it was a wake-up call that didn't completely wake me up. Two years later I had a stroke. I was at Eileen's flat and felt I had to lay down on the couch. There was a searing stinging pain above my eye and then my vision just went. I knew I was in trouble. I was left with damaged muscles in my eye and I was paralysed down the left side for a while. Slowly but surely with the help of excellent medical professionals and the love of my family and friends I recovered and within a couple of years the damage wreaked by the stroke was barely noticeable. I had been very lucky. It did mean we had to postpone our wedding in St Lucia by several months. It happened in the end though in 1998. Thank God.

Mark St John, a hippy lawyer, entered the Bay City Rollers' orbit in the late 1990s. He provided a much-needed boost to us all. He got us talking again for one, especially Les and Eric, and claimed and believed he could help us get back the millions owed to us. In fact, it was not getting it back as we had never had it in the first place. Mark launched a war of words, citing some ambitious targets as to what we felt was due. He rubbished the record company claims that they hadn't been able to pay us because we in the band couldn't agree on who would get what. They could have just handed over the money and let us scrap over it. Arista, now owned by Sony, also tried to get the case thrown out under statutes of limitation. Or in other words – it's so long ago we don't think we should have to pay what you are owed. Mark also got us various gigs insisting we were paid up front. I remember he arranged for us to appear on a TV programme somewhere and promptly divvied up several thousand pounds in notes. That was a novelty.

One of our early fans, and later a successful journalist Caroline Sullivan, released a book called *Bye Bye Baby* about her adolescent years traipsing around America and beyond following the band. The subtitle 'My Tragic Love Affair with the Bay City Rollers' says it all. It was an incisive insight into the minds and obsessions of some Roller fans and our slide from the pinnacle. Caroline records it forensically. It was not comfortable reading for a Bay City Roller.

The book was a success and well received, and Courtney Love wanted to make it into a film. Courtney had been a major fan in her youth, it seems, and fancied producing films. There were all sorts of rumours about Ewan McGregor playing Les and Leonardo DiCaprio being Woody. No mention, sadly, of who might play me. I was scared to pick up the paper in case they decided on Danny De Vito.

Mark was instrumental in getting us to perform together in the UK, for the first time in some years, at the Millennium Hogmanay knees up on December 31, 1999. We played to a huge crowd, estimated to be 180,000, in Princes Street Gardens and we were well received and enjoyed it. At least I did. To feel the love was reassuring and comforting after all of this time. I now know that there was a wonderful symmetry to the evening because it was at the Princes Street bandstand that Derek, Neil and I made our very first public performance all those years ago. I entered the new century as a newly and very happily married man, my love for the band I had formed over 30 years earlier reawakened.

It wasn't all an upward curve from thereon. I had another heart attack and was facing the fact that I was not a young man anymore – the slow realisation of that and one's mortality is not pleasant, but you get used to it. Excitement over the Hogmanay concert and plans to re-form seriously, record and tour washed away. Les published an autobiography that laid bare some of the long-running bad feeling between some of the guys and lifted the lid on Roller life, busting a few myths along the way. Les admitted to having drink and drug problems. Our legal battles grumbled on.

To add to the band's woes, my brother Derek was accused, charged and pleaded guilty to possessing child pornography. Derek believes he was the victim of a set-up vindictively orchestrated by Tam Paton. Our former manager had been increasingly threatening as the band came back together and it looked like our legal action (Tam was not a party to the case) may bear considerable fruit. He couldn't cope with the thought that his boys might have a happy ending when he didn't.

Derek's defence was although he was guilty of possessing child pornography it wasn't his and he didn't know what it was when it was left at his property. The judge in the case acknowledged 'substantial mitigating factors' and sentenced him to only 300 hours of community service.

The nursing regulatory body also investigated Derek's case and concluded he was a fit and proper person to be a nurse and was permitted to carry on in his profession and this he did for the rest of his working life. During his career he gained a Bachelor of Science with distinction in Nursing. Not a bad achievement for a kid who left school at 14 with no qualifications to his name.

Over the years Derek and others have pieced together what happened to him. I said Tam Paton was a good man gone bad, Derek is understandably harsher saying he was a good man turned evil, drunk on the power of the money he was making from being one of Lothian's leading drug barons. One day Derek will prove his innocence and be able to detail Tam's and others' roles in the whole sordid affair.

Tam Paton died from a suspected heart attack whilst in the bath at his home in 2009. He had made his three score years and ten despite his massive weight and suffering two heart attacks and a stroke. Despite this man having stolen much of our money and slipping into a life of depraved debauchery, I felt pangs of sadness. Perhaps it was a reminder to me of my own mortality. Tam was not that far in front of me, after all. However, I had no desire to attend his funeral. Nobby Clark, I understand, was the only Roller that did. Les McKeown did not mince his words, as usual.

'I can't imagine man or beast will be mourning his passing,' he declared.

There were varying reports of how much Tam left in his will ranging from £2m to £5m. Tam was canny if nothing else and whatever he left in his will at the mercy of inheritance taxes would have been a small portion of his actual wealth. He would have used a web of companies and offshore vehicles to shelter his money, I have no doubt of that. That coupled with the age-old Scottish savings vehicle – under the mattress. In his case he would have made sure he could negotiate that web, not like the myriad of schemes set up for us. Little Kellerstain and the properties he owned in Edinburgh city centre alone would have come to a few million pounds.

His final years were miserable, I'm sure. Tam was fighting off various sexual assault allegations in that last decade of life. He gave interviews regularly in the press and on TV. He was bitter (God knows why), forever sniping at one or other of us. We were failures. We were talentless, and it was only his drive and skill that delivered success for us. He was rich. He had settled with the record company. He said these things to try and bait us. It was like a scorned love situation. But, I for one, would not enter a war of words with him. He was a powerful and vindictive man not to be taken lightly. He had friends in high and low places. The friends in high places included politicians and senior members of the police and judiciary. The friends in low places included scum that would slash your face for a bag of Tam's finest Colombian cocaine. A dangerous combination. Paton was convicted of drug supply offences in 2004. He was capable of ruining lives and I believe that he did just that. Time will show Tam Paton to be a far darker force than even we currently believe.

Meanwhile, I had celebrated my 60th birthday in 2008. It's a landmark birthday for sure. I considered sending out a press release saying that Tam Paton was right after all, that I was really only 53. We had a lovely party in my local pub in Bannockburn and I spoilt it all by getting up on stage and singing *Shang-A-Lang*. It was a lovely day opening a golden decade for me.

In 2010, I was approached by the *Daily Mail* who told me that there was a man living out on the Costa Blanca in Spain pretending to me. Apparently, he was dining out, literally, on my name and cadging drinks around the bars in exchange for inside stories of the Bay City Rollers and their excesses and adventures. By all accounts he was my double although they never produced a picture. The *Mail* asked me how I felt. I had just been made redundant as a Byelaws Inspector and was feeling sorry for myself and joked that I felt like going out to Spain and pretending to be him.

18

And I Ran With The Gang

IN 2012, I was invited to see a play in Edinburgh called *And They Played Shang-A-Lang* at the Edinburgh fringe. It was produced by a lovely, clever and creative guy called Liam Rudden who also moonlighted as the entertainments editor of the *Edinburgh Evening News*. Although the show was not about the Rollers, it was very good. Eileen, Liam and myself adjourned to the bar afterwards and had a long chat and Liam revealed that he always wanted to do a production around the Bay City Rollers and asked if I was interested in getting involved. I told him thanks, but no thanks. It had now been 12 years since I'd walked on to a stage at the millennium gig and had barely picked up a guitar since. The very thought of it terrified me.

Liam was charmingly persistent and more specific about what he had in mind. A show about my life from plumber to Roller and back. He sketched out how it could work with actors playing me, whilst I only had to come on stage for a couple of numbers and perhaps do a question and answer session at the end. I could see it. I could see it might work but who'd want to sit through a whole show about me? Who'd even remember me? I turned Liam down again.

When Liam rung again in 2014, I had retired from plumbing. Eileen could hear my indecisiveness and she was getting fed up with me at home, under her feet.

'He'll do it,' she told Liam. The play was to be called *And I Ran With The Gang*.

From there, it went so fast. Liam wrote a great script based on just one three-hour conversation and we were due to open within weeks at the Le Monde Hotel in time for the Edinburgh Festival 2014. It was a small, but highly respected venue in the room called Dirty Martini, catering for around a hundred plus people, but that made it even more personal and special. Some nights we ended up packing in 130. The play was in three parts: my story with a young actor playing me, a Q&A session, and a performance with a brilliant young band playing a medley of the all the hits with me, and sometimes special guests, joining in.

I had stage fright just doing the rehearsals and on the day of the first night I felt physically sick. I thought to myself 'What am I doing putting myself through all this at my time of life?' I could be at home under Eileen's feet or in the Tartan Arms, my local. I watched the first act and then on cue I walked down through the audience slowly towards the stage. I can't walk fast these days. The spotlight picked me out and the audience started to guess it was me. Then they started to applaud and got out of their seats and gave me the most rousing, warm personal applause I have ever received. I wanted to cry. I had never felt so happy and loved. That first night was a resounding success and the following day the reaction on social media was phenomenal.

The show sold out every night. The following year, in 2015, we went again. This time all the tickets were sold in advance and people were arriving from the USA, Canada, Australia, Germany and Japan. People of all creeds and ages coming together for this exclusive, intimate show. We saw older ladies walk in with the aid of sticks and then at the end up dancing and swaying no stick in sight.

On one occasion, my young granddaughter was in the front row. When the voice-over said, 'And now Alan Longmuir' and this young, handsome fella walked on stage, she cried 'That's not my granddad!'

Les turned up a couple of times and joined me on stage which was just fantastic. The audience on those nights really couldn't believe their luck. I was amazed and humbled that so many people out there would pay money and, in many cases, travel so far to see me and hear about my life.

We've done it every year since and I would like to continue to do so if my legs carry me and if people want it. I cannot thank Liam enough for making an old man very happy. I would also like to thank every single person that has attended. I try to do this on the night. I meet and greet and have selfies with everyone should they wish.

At one of the early shows I was approached by a man of about my age. 'Mr Longmuir,' he said. 'My wife is a massive fan of yours. Would you meet her? She's too shy to ask but she's adored you for nearly 40 years.' I looked over and saw this lady standing nervously in the background. She saw me and quickly looked down at the floor. I waved her over. She looked up at me and burst into tears. I hugged her and patted her back. She almost had me at it. It was at times like this when I fully appreciated the powerful effect the band and the music had on a generation. It wasn't just us, and I'm only guessing, but I think we remind many fans of happier times. When they were free, life was easy and a mad adventure of discovery. I think it reminds them of mums and dads perhaps no longer here, friends that have flown, the pleasure and the pain of adolescence and when they come face to face with one of us it's like a key unlocking all those emotions.

At another show there was a similar situation: a husband said would I meet his wife. Of course, I would. This lady was more forthright: 'Aw Alan. How lovely to meet you. You're still as handsome as ever. Aw I just cannae believe it. When you came on Alan I screamed so hard my teeth shot out and then I pissed myself.'

'Nae bother.'

Someone down my local suggested I charge £20 for selfies and signatures.

'You're joking, I hope,' I retorted. 'These people have travelled from all over, paid hard-earned money to come. I wouldnae dream of it. These people put me here. I should be paying them.'

We've taken the show to Toronto twice and there's been talk of coming to London. We'll see. If it all stops tomorrow, it's been one of the most satisfying periods of my career and life thanks to Liam and Eileen.

John McLaughlin came along around the same time as Liam and has been equally responsible for the sweet uplift in the quality of my life I have experienced this century. John is a highly respected musician, song-writer, producer and manager who launched boy band 911 to great success and went on to work with and write songs for Westlife, Busted, Mark Owen and scores of others. Simon Cowell spotted his talent and enlisted him to coach, develop and write for some of his protégés.

Late in 2013 John won one of his many music awards and when interviewed afterwards he was asked was there anything in particular he'd like to achieve that he hadn't already.

'The thing I'd love most of all would be the Bay City Rollers, who I'd love to get back together and in the studio – I mean a proper reunion, a proper band. Imagine making the new Bay City Rollers record. I'd love that more than anything. They've always been my favourite band, so it would just be unbelievable,' he replied.

This was like music to Les McKeown's ears who read the article in a paper. He was soon on the phone to John. They got on like a house on fire and Woody was contacted. Woody got on to me and although I was sceptical at first – not about John but about another attempt at reforming the Rollers – I went to meet John. He's a small guy, John but he has an enormous energy and enthusiasm. You cannot help but like him and be swept along by his optimism, confidence, professionalism and determination. I was in. Eric and Derek decided not to be part of the reunion.

After many meetings, discussions and negotiations we announced the reformation of the Bay City Rollers in September 2015. I wasn't sure what to expect. Whether there would be a resounding 'And?' or even a total dismissal? But, no, the media in Scotland, England, and even worldwide, lapped it up. Les, Stu and I did the rounds of the TV studios. Les and Woody did most of the talking. I was again bemused that the likes of Holly Willoughby and Phillip Schofield saw fit to put us on their shows.

A concert at Glasgow's Barrowland venue was announced 20 December and remarkably it was sold out in three minutes. A second date was announced, and it sold out too. Then a third Barrowlands date was added.

John McLaughlin said to me, 'This is Rollermania all over again.' He had us record a Christmas album and release a single.

Dates at the Hammersmith Apollo also sold out in a flash and our own Usher Hall. Gigs were added in Manchester, the SSE Hydro and other cities. We were touring again. Everywhere we went we played to packed arenas and went down a storm. It was unbelievable. I was 67 years old! The council had decided I was too old to be a Byelaws Inspector. My bones had decided I was too old to be a jobbing plumber. Yet here I was rocking on stage to an enthusiastic audience of mothers, many who had brought their grown-up children and, dare I say it, grandchildren. That first gig at Barrowlands was stupendous. It was a love-in. Nobody was really appreciating the finer points of the music and stagecraft, which was probably a godsend as it was my first time playing to a paying crowd for 15 years, they were there to roll back the years. Nostalgia is a very powerful force.

The *Scotsman* noted:

> *Saturday Night*, the glorious teenage rampage that broke them in America is still their most euphoric moment. Their signature song *Shang-A-Lang* combines rough street politics and doo-wah-diddy teenybop pop in one perfect package which, along with their faithful cover of The Four Seasons' *Bye Bye Baby*, more festive than anything in their Christmas set, proved the ideal rallying cry for this fresh, though more contained wave of Rollermania.

The culmination of our rejuvenation was arguably being invited to appear at the T in the Park three-day festival at Strathallan Castle in Kinross in July 2016. We were on a bill that included The Stone Roses, Kaiser Chiefs, Fun Lovin' Criminals and many others. Despite the crowd being generally younger than our traditional fan-base, and likely with more eclectic musical tastes, our set was roundly and enthusiastically appreciated. A modern audience that had not been subjected to the negative narrative that followed us in many quarters in the 1970s and 1980s saw us for what we were – a good-time band singing good-time songs for people to have a good time to.

But, of course, we are the Bay City Rollers and when we see a good thing we know how to ruin it. Tensions backstage were rearing their ugly head again. The three of us went on STV's *Live At Five* to promote our upcoming concert. Pre-interview Les decided to whip out his solo CD called *Lost Songs* and it was nearly a lost CD as Woody took umbrage and snatched it from Les's hands and tossed it across the studio. Woody then left the interview.

Les later commented: 'I'll make sure Woody has a signed copy in his Christmas stocking. Deep down we'll always be pals.'

Woody had problems with both Les and me, and had said the T in the Park concert would be his last. We managed to muddle through until the Hydro concert in December 2016. That was our last. But never say never.

In 2016 they unveiled a plaque at Ryrie's Bar on Dalry Road close to our family home. It says home to the Bay City Rollers but in truth I was the only one that ever drank in there. But my dad did as well, so I guess that makes it as close to the birthplace of the Rollers you might get. Derek and I turned up at the unveiling in a white Rolls Royce. It was a thrill for us brothers to be together and be appreciated by so many loyal and local fans. I'm told the plaque has become a bit of a pilgrimage destination for committed Rollers' fans and that's a lovely feeling for us Longmuirs. Thanks are due to Graeme Whitehead for running a campaign for a plaque in our home town.

Another pleasant interlude these days is my annual visit from a group of ladies we all call The Tartanettes. They are committed Bay City Rollers fans from wide and far who have never given up the faith and we all eat and drink together in the Tartan Arms bar and restaurant. I am forever touched and humbled that these charming ladies make the effort to come every year from their domestic nests to spend a few hours with me. This is 40 years on. It's lovely to be loved. Thank you so much, all of you.

Finally, in 2016, we reached an out-of-court settlement with Sony, who now own the Arista and Bell assets, over our unpaid royalties. We didn't receive a great deal each – enough for some nice holidays but not life-changing. But, for me, it was a huge relief and a triumph. It was always there like a throbbing head in the background and now it was over. It meant we were vindicated. We *were* owed that money. We *were* treated badly. We *were* right to fight for what was ours. The fact that it had been whittled away to almost nothing by professional fees and god knows what else is a shame. A great shame, but as I have said before we were wee fairground goldfish swimming among sharks. Now we wouldn't have to watch helplessly as our songs were packaged, diced and cut and released in countries all over the world knowing none of the value of the sales they generated would accrue to us. Although financially it was painful, it was more humiliating. To think people could take our work, blatantly sell it and we could do nothing about it.

One of the most frequent questions I am asked is what happened to the Rollers' millions? We will never know, for sure and there has been books and documentaries devoted to the subject, but my take is this:

- We, the band, spent far more than we ever realised. First class travel, limos, posh hotels and the expenses of five young 'superstars' does not come cheap.

- We were handed out money for cars and houses and living. So, although not much relative to the amounts being generated, it is untrue that we never saw a penny.

- Tam Paton feathered his nest in the early years in salaries, commissions and backhanders before any notional amounts reached the 'pot'. The total of this could have been substantial.

- When Tam realised he was out of his depth he/we hired outside 'expertise'. These included some dodgy white-collar types on both sides of the Atlantic. I believe most of the money was 'lost' here. I think an army of accountants, lawyers and consultants feasted themselves on our money in the quest to 'find' our money. Of course, there were some honest professionals among them.

- The merchandise sales were poorly managed and huge amounts of revenue were generated for cowboys with no connection to the Rollers.

If the record companies had simply paid us normally then we would never have needed to hire these people in the first place. That is, or was, a music industry thing. There is a barely a successful act out there who have not had issues with their management or record companies and have had to hire lawyers to squeeze out what they are owed or even resort to court action. The Beatles, The Rolling Stones, The Kinks, Gilbert O'Sullivan, Michael Jackson and George Michael spring to mind.

Now, though, a blockage has been cleared and royalties should flow, which is something. I'm hoping someone will make a new blockbuster film called *Bye Bye Baby* and use all our songs as the soundtrack. Hopefully, long, long after I've gone a cheque will drop every six months through the front doors of my loved ones. It might not be much. But they might think 'Good old, Alan. He's got us a pint or two there.'

And that is where I am today, in a very lovely place. I play occasional gigs with Les's Legendary Bay City Rollers and I absolutely adore it. The reception we get is magnificent and the fans wrap us up in a blanket of love. Many were there in the 1970s and there is a bond of that shared experience of something very special that neither they, or we, ever fully understood. Les and I exchange warm smiles on stage and know that, for all the ups and downs, we love each other too. And best of all, he pays me.

So, with the love of my family, the confidence, love and support of Liam Rudden with the *I Ran With The Gang* show, and Martin Knight becoming a friend and having the patience, belief and skills to help me write my life story, my twilight years are proving to be a voyage of joyous discovery. It would be the icing on this wonderful cake if us creaking old Rollers could lay our ghosts to rest, rise above all the old rubbish and come together one last time and not let the music die. That would delight me. After all, we are not getting younger and one of us will be the first to go, and statistically that's me!

I would like to end this book with a heartfelt thank you to all of you – the fans. I don't think the term fans does you justice. You were all individuals who saw us wee boys from Scotland and took us into your hearts wherever you were in the world and locked us in there through thick and thin, across the decades. Many of you have become personal friends and I like to think we are all part of a special global family. I cannot describe adequately what that devotion and loyalty means to this wizened old plumber from Edinburgh. Thank you! Bless you! Keep on dancing.

Epilogue

THE LAST TIME I saw Alan was the last of three consecutive taping sessions in his friend's house in Bannockburn in May 2018. We were coming to the end of the book and had been talking about some dark days in Alan's life and then how love and happiness had washed over him again. He wanted to tell me more about Eileen, his wife, his stepchildren and his grandchildren. He wanted to talk about Jordan, his son by Jan, his first wife. He wondered how much plumbing we could get in the book.

'I finished a Byelaws Inspector, you know.'

Alan had told me this many times. He seemed prouder of this than all manner of gold discs, or for filling stadiums worldwide, or for creating the biggest band in the world for a time.

'Not sure the readers will want to read too much about plumbing.'

He nodded.

'Aye, you may be right. Interesting, though.'

He wanted a 'selfie' for his Facebook page although I suspected he had little idea of what Facebook was and how it worked. He was looking forward to the 2018 run of *I Ran With The Gang* although he said he was nervous. I pointed out it was now well established and a resounding success there was nothing to be nervous about.

'I just worry aboot things,' he explained.

'But there's nothing to worry about.'

'I know.'

He praised Liam Rudden and said Liam had given him back his confidence. He said he was looking forward to some more gigs with Les.

He asked me about George Best who I had written a book with. What was he like? I said he was a quiet, humble man too. 'Like yourself,' I said. Alan smiled.

'I'd like to have met him.'

'Surely, you must have?'

'Aye, I think he may have been in Stringfellows once in the 1980s when I was in there with Duncan Faure. But I wouldnae introduce myself. Never in a million years.'

Alan told me about his upcoming Mexico holiday. He was going with Eileen to mark his 70th birthday. I told him to be careful what he ate after his food poisoning episode in Cuba a year earlier where he and Eileen had booked a top-notch holiday and found themselves dumped in a dilapidated hotel where cockroaches shared their breakfast. Alan picked up a food poisoning bug and ended being taken off the homeward airplane in a wheelchair. We both laughed. We arranged to meet again when he came back to go over the book and add some plumbing stories. Alan assured me they would be hilarious.

His friend Alastair came to collect me in his car. Alan had arranged for Alastair to kindly take me back to the railway station. As we prepared to pull away he emerged from his friend's house after having locked it up. Alan Longmuir stood in the road, looking one way and the next. In his flat cap and coat, nobody would have guessed there stood a man who'd been to Hollywood and back.

'What's he doing?' I asked.

'He's deciding whether to go home or go to the pub,' said Alastair.

We both agreed that he looked a bit frail and vulnerable standing there. That was my last image of Alan.

In June I received the shocking news that Alan had been taken seriously ill and was in a critical condition in hospital in Cancun, Mexico. A virus had attacked his vital organs and it was clear his life was in imminent danger. After some days he was returned home to Scotland by air ambulance. Because he hadn't died I convinced myself he wouldn't and that he'd recover. He sent a message to me via Eileen not to worry and that the book would go ahead come what may. It was heart-breaking he was thinking of others at a time of such personal peril. Besides his close family, I know Liam Rudden and Les McKeown went to see him.

On Monday 2 July an email landed in my inbox from Derek Longmuir. He informed me that Alan had died peacefully at 6am that morning in the Forth Valley Hospital. Although I was expecting this news at some time it was still a shock and I felt bereft. I had only known Alan for six months and met him relatively few times but nevertheless had become very fond of him. I, too, had looked forward to the book coming out and the two of us touring media outlets and attending functions. I had hoped to become close friends after the book stuff had died down and I am sure we would have.

That Monday I had to drive somewhere. I was on the motorway listening to Radio 2. Jeremy Vine interrupted his phone-in flow to say how very sorry he was to hear of the passing of Alan Longmuir. He mentioned having met the Bay City Rollers somewhere when they were past their peak.

'Do you admit to being a Bay City Rollers fan?' he asked, solemnly. 'I do.'

And he played *Bye Bye Baby*. Then I cried.

Alan would have been flabbergasted at the immediate reaction to his death. It was on national television and radio bulletins and most newspapers across the world ran the story. Social media was awash with condolences, memories and tributes. So many from people who met or knew him personally. The hash tag *#ByeByeAlan* was trending on Twitter. He really would not have believed it. It's so sad because I am convinced, as each year passes, the silly musical snobbery and prejudice that the Bay City Rollers suffered is flaking away and what is left is an appreciation and fondness of a really good band that made millions very happy and provided the soundtrack to so many young lives. Alan's pivotal role in that is being recognised more and more.

He would have been even more astonished at the widespread obituaries and tributes that appeared as the sad news sank in. BBC Radio 4 included him in its *Last Word* feature of weekly deaths. Obituaries appeared in *The Times*, *The Guardian*, *The Los Angeles Times*, *The Herald*, *The Scotsman*, *New York Times*, *Sydney Morning Herald* and *Japan Today*, to name just a few. Alan really was international news again. In Scotland, the outpouring of grief and memories was intense and heartfelt. The *Edinburgh Evening News* devoted a front page and a six-page colour tribute. Demand for the issue was such that the paper gave out a special telephone number for people ordering copies.

Les McKeown was one of the first of Alan's contemporaries to pay tribute:

They were fantastic, crazy days. We all seemed to get on well with each other and we were on a mission to make the Bay City Rollers – and tartan – famous all over the world. And we managed to do that. We turned the world tartan back in the 1970s. Alan was always a total gentleman – very humble. He was everybody's favourite because of his demeanour. He always signed people's autograph books. A true gent.

Eric Faulkner added:

Words are not enough. Rest in peace, Alan. Be still in the solace of your sleep. May your spirit run free.

Nobby Clark observed:

He was the coolest guy. Alan Longmuir always had style. RIP.

Also, these:

'I was proud to have known, worked with and called him a friend,' John McLaughlin.

'Thank you for the wonderful music that lives on. A wonderful guy who always said he was just an Edinburgh plumber who got lucky,' Randy Bachman of The Guess Who and Bachman Turner Overdrive.

Dave Valentine of The Hipple People, who knew Alan from back in those formative Edinburgh club days commented: 'Alan had no airs or music claptrap about him, he was just a nice regular guy who loved being in a band, little did he know the journey it would take him on.'

Even Johnnie Walker, the disc jockey who in the 1970s had refused to play Bay City Rollers music and threatened to resign if he was forced to, did exactly that on his '70s radio show and paid a nice tribute to Alan. That would have warmed Alan's heart.

On Thursday 12 July 2018 Bannockburn buried its famous resident. The funeral service was held at the Allan Church which was also that very day celebrating its 150th anniversary. *Morning Has Broken* and *Abide with Me* were the hymns that sandwiched tributes from Nik Rankin, Alan's stepson and Liam Rudden, producer of Alan's musical show. Both eulogies affectionately captured Alan's humour, humility and honour. Liam told a story of how Alan would sit outside the Le Monde Hotel while his *I Ran With The Gang* play was showing, and he'd sit on a chair, with his flat cap pulled down, reading a paper as the crowds passed by looking at the life-size poster of a much younger Alan he was sitting in front of. It gave him a mischievous pleasure to hear their comments. Nik recalled how whenever his step-dad was left alone with the grandkids, he and his wife would return home to find Alan covered in make-up, his remaining hair all over the place. He just could not say no to the children.

The church was full and of course there was raw grief especially among the close family and friends but for me there was an overriding sense of peace, goodwill and appreciation of a good man's life. It was like Alan himself had influenced the day. He would have wanted nae bother and everyone to focus on the good times and to look forward. Especially look forward. He was not one for living in the past or regretting it. He never bore grudges, only goodwill.

Nobby Clark was there as was Peko, Les McKeown's Japanese wife, representing her husband who was touring Australia with his band. Rumour had it that Eric Faulkner had set out to the funeral but took ill. I feel sure other figures from the band's past stole in and out not wishing to attract attention.

I chatted to a man in the pew behind who told me he had led the campaign for a plaque that ended up being mounted in Ryrie's, the bar near the

Longmuir family home. He said he was a massive fan from back in the 1970s. He could see some surprise and that I was under the impression that male Rollers fans were a rare thing. There were plenty, he assured me, and he rolled up his sleeve to show me his tattoo – *Don't Let the Music Die*, the same record emanating from the church speakers as we waited for the service to begin.

As the mourners stepped outside into the sunlight photographers and journalists stood across the road – a small reminder of those manic Roller days. If he was able to do so Alan would have stopped and given them the pictures they wanted. The cortège walked slowly up the street towards Bannockburn cemetery led by a lone piper. It was a memorable sight. In scenes I have not witnessed since I was a small child, I noticed the High Street shops had closed and shoppers and staff alike were lining the route. The RBS staff had draped a tartan rug over the barrier outside their branch. As we turned into the cemetery itself, I hoped that the piper would strike up *Bye Bye Baby*, but that could have been a tune too far.

Back at the Tartan Arms, friends and family gathered in the back bar where Alan was to have held his 70th birthday celebrations on his return from Mexico. A friend took the microphone and revealed that a ticket Alan had bought before his departure had won the sweepstake. Alan would have loved the irony. The pal also told of how they would go fishing together and one day Alan turned up on the riverbank and his friend noticed one shoe Alan was wearing was a brogue. The other was not. He pointed this out. Alan looked down at his feet.

'Aye,' said Alan. 'I've got another pair the same at home.'

After Alan died, but before the funeral, I was alone in the cottage in Norfolk where I go to write. It is in a remote area where mobiles rarely work, sometimes it's hard to get a television signal. Because of this I am rarely disturbed. Suddenly my phone broke the silence and it made me jump. I was writing this epilogue. When I looked at the handset vibrating on the chair next to me the name Alan Longmuir was flashing up. My stomach turned over and my throat drained out.

Alan rang me a lot. He was excited by the book but often he just rang. He'd chat about the show, the weather, the grandchildren, the guys in the pub. He rarely mentioned the Bay City Rollers. He was phoning about nothing in particular. It was like he just wanted to you to know he was thinking of you. I found out later he was making similar calls to other friends and family members.

My brain temporarily could not process the telephone call. Dead people don't normally ring you up. I was too scared to pick up the handset and just stared over at it wide-eyed as it went to voicemail. I warily picked up the mobile and listened to the message and it was Alan's stepson, Nik introducing himself, calling on Alan's phone, and beginning the long process of attending to his dad's affairs. I had been wondering and worrying slightly that morning when would be an appropriate time to speak to Alan's family. I know that wasn't physically Alan calling but I am convinced he was guiding the call and putting my mind at rest.

Another issue in connection with the book had not been discussed in any detail and I was in a quandary over that too, a tad lost without Alan's guidance and at the funeral it was resolved after a chance conversation. Alan was behind that too.

He was determined to get his story out there. It had become very important to him and now I think he may have known his life may have been coming to an end. On a social media clip he recorded shortly before his death he said that this year's *I Ran With The Gang* would probably be his last. Of the book he said more than once that he wanted to get it down on paper and out before 'it was too late'. People talk like this, I know, but I do wonder.

What a life the man had! He'd experienced highs and lows beyond most people's imagination. He impacted on so many other lives it's hard to comprehend. He managed to achieve so much in his 70 years. He walked with kings but never lost the common touch. Yet, to get him to reveal any of this let alone appreciate it was like getting blood out of a stone. It is a mark of the man that I never heard or read a bad word about him. The most used word spoken and written to describe him was simple, but never more apt – lovely. Alan was a lovely man. He will be sorely missed. Like all the good entertainers, and all the good people, Alan Longmuir left us all – family, friends, fans – wanting more.

End Piece

Where Will I Be Now?

Ann-Margret
Works regularly as an actress on US television.

Ayshea
Married a US record executive and disappeared from view.

Barrow, Tony
Our former PR man died in 2016 aged 80. Tony spent many years with The Beatles before representing us via his company. He is widely credited with coining the 'Fab Four' name for The Beatles.

Bee Gees
Are now The Bee Gee following the sad deaths of twins Maurice and Robin Gibb. I feel for poor Barry losing three brothers (Andy being the other, much earlier) so prematurely.

Bernstein, Sid
Died in 2013 at the grand age of 95.

Blaikley, Alan
Went on to write the Adrian Mole musical among many other things. For some years worked as a psychotherapist. His time with us probably gave him a grounding in that profession.

Bolan, Marc
Tragically died in a car accident in 1977. His day would most certainly have come again had he lived.

Brush, Basil
Lives quietly in Brinsworth House, Twickenham, a residential home for retired theatre and entertainment professionals.

Calder, Tony
Died in 2018 aged 74. After his brush with us Tony went on to have significant success with Eddy Grant and then Jive Bunny.

Cassidy, David
We shared many a girl's bedroom wall with David. He sadly died from liver failure in 2017.

Castle Campbell Hotel, The
Continued to trade under many owners until 2014 when it finally closed. I heard it sold in 2018 for around £300,000 to developers who have applied to convert the building into flats.

Clark, Nobby
Wrote his autobiography in 2014 where he recounts his Roller career and subsequent personal battles and recovery. Nobby has recently hosted his own radio show in Edinburgh and has recorded albums, some produced by his former Rollers' colleague, Davie Paton.

Cohen, Norman
Died just a couple of years after producing *Burning Rubber* at only 47 years old. Hopefully, there was no connection.

Connery, Sean
Now moving in fast on his 90th birthday, he lives in splendid retirement in the Bahamas. I wonder if he ever thinks of Terry, our old St. Cuthbert's milk round horse.

Cosell, Howard
In 1980 he interrupted a live football commentary to announce the death of John Lennon to millions of viewers. The Muppets had a recurring character, Louis Kazagger, a sportscaster with nasal inflection that was based on Cosell. He died in 1995.

Crewe, Bob
Died in 2014. I am forever grateful to him for co-writing that wonderful song *Bye Bye Baby*.

Crofft, Sid and Marty
Are both still with us and, despite Sid pushing 90, are still working.

Davis, Clive
Ended up one of the most powerful music executives of all time working with just about everyone. He is still the chief creative officer at Sony at 86 years of age.

Dee, Dave
Became a Justice of the Peace in later life. Dave died in 2009, aged 67.

Denning, Chris
In 2016 Denning was jailed after admitting sexual offences against young boys.

Duncan, Jake
Went on to become the biggest name in tour management. He has worked with (among scores of others) Aerosmith, George Michael, Ossie Osbourne, Bruce Springsteen and more recently Paul Potts and Little Mix.

Dunn, Alan
Married and last seen carpet-fitting in Dundee.

Epstein, Brian
Died of from a drugs overdose in 1967.

Faulkner, Eric
Has performed with his own band including a set at Glastonbury. In 2015 Eric fell ill with viral encephalitis but thankfully has gradually recovered.

Faure, Duncan
Was inducted into the Rock Godz Hall of Fame in Las Vegas in 2014. In 1988 he provided backing vocals on Madonna's *Who's That Girl*. In 2017 he toured South Africa where he remains a legendary musical figure. Duncan now lives in Las Vegas with his wife and children and has said his time with the Rollers were the best years of his life.

Frechter, Colin
Last heard of living in the West Country of England after some years in Spain.

Gaudio, Bob
Bob has deservedly been inducted into the Songwriters Hall of Fame. *Jersey Boys* the musical about him and his friends' lives is the best couple of hours that can be spent in a theatre.

Glitter, Gary
Managed to make a comeback in the 1980s but was jailed for 16 years in 2015 for sexual offences against young girls.

Goodison, Johnny
Co-writer of *Give A Little Love* with Phil Wainman sadly had a heart attack and died many years ago.

Gray, Les
Les semi-retired to Portugal but sadly had a heart attack while fighting throat cancer and died in 2004. He was only 57.

Henderson, Neil
Carried on playing with Middle of the Road into the 1980s and beyond.

Henry, Stuart
Stuart died in 1995 after a long and brave battle with MS.

Howard, Ken
Ken has not been idle in recent years. He has produced films and documentaries and written books and developed successful board games.

King, Jonathan
Although he vehemently protests his innocence, King has served time for sexual activity with underage boys.

Knievel, Evel
Perhaps the most remarkable thing about this daredevil's life is that he died from natural causes in 2007.

Leahy, Dick
Went on to have an even more successful career in the music business most notably with Wham! and George Michael as a solo artist.

Lyall, Billy
Sadly, died in 1989 from AIDS-related illnesses, aged just 36. In his autobiography for some reason Tam Paton insists on spelling Billy's surname as Lyl.

Martin, Bill
I met Bill recently when he came to see the *And I Ran With The Gang* show at the Edinburgh Fringe. We had a lovely chat and catch-up. He said to me that he and Phil Coulter really should have let the Rollers have had their head and apologised for stifling us artistically. He added in a BBC documentary: 'These wee boys should have had everything.'

McCartney, Paul
Remains one of the best musicians on the planet. My admiration for him never wanes. I think he has taken stick over the years because he is here and John Lennon isn't.

McGlynn, Pat
Still lives in the Edinburgh area and has been involved in property development.

Mitchell, Ian
Ian is now living in California where he works as a computer programmer and motivational speaker. Over the years he has played in various Rollers-related bands. Ian enjoys a staunch and devoted following among many Rollers fans.

Monkees, The
Reformed and toured more than once after they disbanded for the first time in 1971. Like us, they found their loyal fans never lost their appetite for them. Tragically, vocalist Davy Jones died at 66 in 2012.

Nash, Robin
The dapper producer of *Top of the Pops* went on to produce sitcoms *Terry and June* and *Bread*. He died in 2011, aged 84.

Newton-John, Olivia
Settled with her record company over unpaid royalties from the *Grease* soundtrack in 2006. Despite suffering illness, Olivia still tours. She remains beautiful.

Nichol, Ian
Former member of The Hipple People sadly died in 2012 of a brain tumour.

Noone, Peter
Stayed in America and became a naturalised citizen. He looks more than 13 now, but not a lot.

O'Sullivan, Gilbert
Lives quietly on the island of Jersey.

Pascal, Olivia
Still acts in her native country of Germany. I like to think she yearns to make a sequel to *Burning Rubber* with me.

Paterson, Linnie
Inexplicably, never made the big time. He died in his 40s from asbestosis contracted during his years working as a welder.

Paton, Davie
Has enjoyed a varied and illustrious career working with The Alan Parsons Project, Elton John and Kate Bush. He also played on one of the bestselling singles of all time – *Mull of Kintyre* by Paul McCartney.

Peel, John
Didn't live to be 200 years old, passing away in 2004, aged 65.

Perkins, Barry
Died in Bournemouth in 2014, he was 77. Some reports claim he had been cab-driving in his later years.

Porteous, Neil
Remained my friend for the rest of his life. He never regretted leaving the Rollers. He stayed married to Fiona and they had a wonderful daughter. In 1990 a mini-cab business he was involved in ran into financial difficulties and, inexplicably, dear Neil took his own life. He thought everyone would be better off without him. We're not, Neil. You've left a bloody great hole. Every day I miss his sense of humour and just knowing he's around.

Raspberry, Larry
Former lead singer of The Gentrys who first recorded *Keep on Dancing*, developed an acting career and appeared in the film *This Is Elvis*.

Richard, Cliff
Was growing his own wine in Portugal. He obviously doesn't drink too much of it because now, at nearly 80, he looks little different from the day he was bundled into a van to act as a decoy for us outside the Granada TV studios.

Stigwood, Robert
Spent much of his later years living on the Isle of Wight. Despite this he managed to live to 81, passing away in 2016.

Valentine, Dave
Still leads The Hipple People to this day. It was wonderful to see him after all this time when he coincidentally walked into my local just a couple of years ago. More so, because he was with Colin Chisholm of Bilbo Baggins, another Tam-managed, Edinburgh band.

Wainman, Phil
Went on to produce *I Don't Like Mondays* for the Boomtown Rats in 1979. In 1999 he said of his relationship with the Rollers: 'I just think we had the chemistry. I gave them what Jonathan King didn't and what Bill Martin and Phil Coulter couldn't. I wanted the best for them and was their perfect ally.'

Wakeman, Rick
Has remained busy since the 1970s. He has been married four times.

Wild, Jack

Found it hard to move his acting career into adult roles despite being an adult. He had episodes of alcoholism and lost much of the fortune he made from his early film successes. He died in 2006, aged just 53.

Wood, Stuart

Has enjoyed a successful post-Roller career producing the debut album of The MacDonald Brothers and other projects. He also plays with his band. Woody produced an autobiographical documentary of his life on DVD, *Rollercoaster*, in 2007.

Wyngarde, Peter

Died in 2018 at 90. Some said he had exaggerated his age downward and was closer to 100.

Young, Muriel

After a very successful television career Muriel retired in 1986. She died in 2001 aged 77. The whereabouts of Ollie Beak and Fred Barker are unknown.

Appendix 1

THE FOLLOWING INTERVIEW was carried out by Caroline Coon and published in *Melody Maker* in 1975. I think it an interesting window on the Rollers at a point in time, when we were in the studio recording our third album *Wouldn't You Like It*. It was a time when we were still attempting to assimilate our huge fame and success and beginning to assert ourselves creatively.

'When anyone slates us, you can bet they've never heard our own stuff – Derek is a brilliant drummer.'

Eric Faulkner is the epitome of a pin-up pop idol. He is a teenage Warren Beatty, highly strung, vulnerable, a dreamer quivering with nervous sensibility. When he poses for photos with the other Rollers, the comparatively rugged brothers Alan and Derek Longmuir (bass and drums), the Jack the Ladish Leslie McKeown (lead vocals) and the mischievous Stuart 'Woody' Wood (guitar), then the romanticism in this cornflower-blue eyes and classically pretty baby-face is magnified beyond a fan's wildest dreams.

Nor is the photographic image an illusion. In the flesh, Eric's chestnut hair has a real shine, his skin is really smooth, his face unspotty, and his nubile beard is shaved perhaps once a week.

He has the sidelong insecure coltishness of a man on the verge of discovering his potential – and 18 months in an increasingly grueling limelight has yet to rub away what remains of his adolescent bloom.

He arrives to be interviewed in the Roller outfit which he invented. The short-sleeved shirt is flapping open (he has no hairs on his chest), and white tartan trimmed trousers caress his lower calf to reveal a generous stretch of striped black, red and yellow sock.

He is shoeless, and he bounces around on his toes like a jerky out of control puppet. Then he crouches uneasily on the edge of a chair looking at me with the belligerent air of a convict who has been brought up from the cells for an interrogation with prosecuting counsel.

And he IS virtually a prisoner. For more than a week the Rollers have been in a secret hideaway, recording their third album.
They record, eat, sleep, in the studio compound.

But if their enforced isolation from bright lights and home
comforts is an infliction to be borne with gritted teeth then the
atmosphere in the studio is consoling and rewarding. There is an
unmistakable, if constrained, feeling of elation in the air.

Shyly the boys have asked producer Phil Wainman to play
some of their half-finished tracks. Wainman obliges. The tape
slips past the playback heads. The sound is terrific. The boys, who
have played together for years, stand around the studio console
feeding off each other's relief and sense of achievement.

They know their next album will be the biggest yet – and
for the first time in their recording careers they have been given
enough studio time to enable them to pay special attention to
individual solos as well as the blanket, mish-mash of sound.

The band's excitement is close to fever pitch. This month they
go to the States and before they play one live note on stage, over
80 million people will have seen them two weeks running on *The
Howard Cosell Show*.

Rollermania has already received more attention in the American national press than the last Rolling Stones tour and Tam
Paton, the band's manager, plans a date for the Rollers at the
massive Shea Stadium next summer.

No wonder Eric looks serious, tense and tired. He massages
his forehead, but he cannot escape this interview nor the enormity
of the future which is bearing down on him.

'This is the last time we'll be in the studio for some time,' he
tells me, making an effort. I ask him to speak more slowly since
he runs his words together and his native Edinburgh brogue is
almost unintelligible. 'This session will get our next album and
possibly our next two singles. We may do some recording in
America though.'

What is the most telling difference between the time he first
went into a recording studio and now?

'Now, if we've got an idea we can try it. Before when we
worked with Martin and Coulter like, we were doing one-night
stands, it was the only way we could survive, so if we had to do
a session we sort of said: 'We can manage the 16th' or something
and then we'd only have aboot five hours. It was always a bit
rushed.'

Was he prepared for his first unedifying experiences in a recording studio? 'No. It was a sort of big industry-type thing which revolved around showbiz and we found ourselves caught in the middle. But we done more on those early records than people think.

'The only thing we never played on was *Keep on Dancing*. Which was, when? I mean I was still at school... everybody slates us aboot that, but we just get a good laugh half the time – because, well, I know more about music than most people of my age. And some that are older as well!'

Eric's prickly defensiveness about his musical ability is understandable. Contrary to popular belief, the band has more than paid its dues.

The Rollers' history goes back eight years to when Alan Longmuir played in a group called the Saxons. When his brother Derek joined, the band changed its name to the Bay City Rollers. They were on the road for two years before a record company showed any interest.

In 1970, Dick Leahy, of Bell, was in Scotland. By chance he missed a plane to Glasgow and decided to spend the evening at a local disco in Edinburgh where the Rollers were playing.

The local kids received the band enthusiastically and the record boss was impressed. They were summoned to London's Olympic Studios.

Too broke to pay for decent hotel rooms the Rollers slept in their van when Jonathan King wasn't getting them to sing along to tracks. For the band, London, a recording studio and a famous producer was a dream come true.

Ken Howard and Alan Blaikley (of Dave, Dee, Dozy, Beaky, Mick and Tich fame) produced the next Rollers single, *Manana*. It won the 1972 International Song Contest in Luxembourg but didn't make it in the UK. The group, exhausted by touring, were on the verge of breaking up. Then Bill Martin and Phil Coulter took over. They produced the single, *Saturday Night* but by October 1973 that, too, was obviously a flop.

'I thought we had really had it then,' Tam Paton told me. 'I went to see Dick Leahy at Bell and to this day I believe he was going to tell me that as far as they were concerned, it was all over. And I was scared. We were deep in debt and I couldnae think what other company would be interested.'

He did a down-on-the-knees job convincing Leahy they had a huge following, a swelling fan club and all they needed was another chance.

'I think Leahy felt sorry for me,' says Tam. The band trekked down to London and recorded Martin and Coulter's *Remember*.

Tam Paton brought a pile of fan club magazine lists complete with addresses and flooded Cassidy and Osmond supporters with photos of the Rollers and an exhortation to buy their new single.

Tam believes this one-man publicity stunt, financed by his mother, made its mark. The single started moving. But when the Rollers appeared on *Top of the Pops* they were still too broke to afford any flashy new outfits. Instead, before they drove to London, they sat up all night at Eric's digs chopping off their trousers bottoms and sewing bits of tartan to their cheap army surplus shirts.

Their impact on *Top of the Pops* electrified the teenage viewers. TV screens all over the country registered the band's uniqueness. For too long teenagers had made do with pop stars, like Gary Glitter and Alvin Stardust, masquerading as their peers behind thick pancake make-up. The Rollers captivated an audience starved of the genuine article. Teenagers now had real teenage idols.

Many people believe the ballyhoo and the talk of Rollermania is unjustifiable and repeatedly slammed for being 'hyped' and 'manufactured.' Nothing could be further from the truth.

The band has had six top ten singles, two top ten albums, a biography which sold more copies in the first week of publication than *The Day of the Jackal*, and their own networked TV show.

They are successful, not because thousands of pounds have been poured into their image – the record company was reluctant to spend any money on them at all – but because they project a convincingly youthful optimism for life, an unjaded dedication to the process of entertainment and they sing distinguished pop anthems which applaud, endorse and pay homage to the teenage state of being.

Eric joined the Rollers four years ago, but when did he first get into music?

'Oh, it all started when I was six. At school we were given a test to see if we had any rhythm. But you're only six years old and so, you know, they can't tell very much. Then I started having violin lessons for about an hour every day. And then I got intae the Edinburgh Schools Orchestra when I was 14. There was a time when I was trying to do that and be in a pop group. I was in Kip and we were bumming around in Ford Transits and all. But being at school, playing the violin and the orchestra and everything started getting a bit much. There were gigs at night and everything.

'So eventually I jacked in the orchestra, I couldnae do both. I've always been intae pop music. I was always lurking in music shops trying out guitars. But when you're 12 you don't think in terms of a career. You just do it. If the Bay City Rollers broke up, I'd just join another group.'

How useful is the bit of classical violin he learned?

'It's great because I can read music. And on a few tracks on this LP we've used cellos and things which I've arranged. When anyone slates us, you can bet your bottom dollar that they've never listened to us doing our own stuff. If they'd take the time to listen they'd know that Derek is a brilliant drummer.'

His indignation against those who cast apprehensions on his musical integrity bubbles to the surface again.

'I'd be the first to say that my violin playing wasn't anything spectacular. But the actual training, to be able to read music and do arrangements was worth it. I still carry chord books around with me. I'm a bit of a swat. One day, when this is all over, I'd like to go off and get a degree and what have you but, at the moment, it's just something I say I'll do one day.'

Is he happy with the way the Rollers play now, or does he want the band to improve?

'What I think the success has done – well, everybody's watching to see if we're just five pretty faces or not. But I know we can do more than everybody gives us credit for. We've just got to go ahead and do it. Then, through time, it will show. I mean there are things on *Once Upon A Star* – our second album – which are really good that people ignore.'

Like what for instance?

'Some of the harmonies. We spent a long time doing them. And there is our song called, *La Belle Jeane* which has mandolins and things on it. But people just think we're a drum-beating, shoowopdewop-band and that's all we can do. Now that we're big, we've got to prove ourselves, but I don't think we have to change. Because, in the end, what we are doing is our best. Of course, we want our music to develop. But what's the point in telling you now that we eventually want to sound like... the Carpenters, or something?'

Eric is shut in hotel rooms for much of the time. Does he get any opportunity to listen to other people's music?

'Oh yes, we carry lots of tapes around with us and I listen to everything and anything. Especially things that are real well produced. Rock 'n' Roll's great, it's good to jump around to, but I prefer music that someone has spent a lot of time producing.'

Since Woody joined the band in 1973, they have written songs together but, as the pressure increases, is he finding the time to write a problem?

'Yes, it was hard during the tour because we knew we had this album to do, we knew we had to have songs ready, but we were rushing here and there, the whole thing was exciting, and so we just didnae have a chance to do anything. But there were a lot of ideas we've had for years which come back.

'And the fact that the group's 'made it' makes it easier. The money's there. Now, if we want something – say if I want a string-machine, I could phone up and buy it. It's easier now to do what we want.

'We've been recording here for eight days and six of the songs we've done are ours.' Pause. 'I'm sorry... I feel embarrassed to talk about OUR songs...'

He's afraid to seem conceited, which he is not, and he baulks at revealing just how seriously he takes his music.

'You see, music is our life,' he continues almost apologetically.

'We've been, always, five guys that enjoy going out on the road doing gigs and that and we've just caught on with the gear and everything and we've been sort of lifted intae a superstar bracket. But we're still the same five guys and we still love music. We'd love to do more gigs, but it's difficult now.'

Does he set out to write commercially or does he write how he feels?

'Yeah! That's a good point! We know that we appeal to a certain market more than others and you've got to accept that. I feel we're holding back some of things we'd like to write. We've got to write commercially at the moment.

'I think our fans expect it and if we changed overnight – which any group can do, it's just a case of going at the whole thing in a different way, using different recording techniques and that – it would be too soon. When you listen to our seventh album then you'll notice the difference.'

Does he feel restricted, having to write the way they do now?

'No, because you can still do commercial things which are good. And anyway, more people listen to you. You can do the most amazing freaky things and only a very small percentage of the people hear you.'

How much control do the Rollers have over the final sound?

'Well, Phil Wainman's a great producer so he's usually right. But we can say what we think, what we don't like, at every stage, and we hear the mixes.

'These sessions have been tremendous so far, but I've got to be fair, we did our first album *Rollin'* in four days. We went intae the studio and batted down the tracks. But that wasnae Phil Coulter's fault. That was the only time we had.

'Everybody thinks the split with him was a big aggro thing, but he wrote four hit songs for us and we're very grateful.'

What about the struggle you had to record your songs?

'Well, yes, that was why we broke up with Martin and Coulter, really. They wanted to do their own songs and we really wanted to do ours. We were caught in a big showbiz thing and the record company couldnae see any reason to break a running winning streak. But then the whole thing gets impersonal and it gets down to money. And we found ourselves inside that.'

Tam and the Rollers fought hard for their own songs and eventually Phil Wainman was brought in to produce them. He doesn't insist on having his own songs on both the A and B sides of singles, but he is a songwriter and I wondered how much help he gives Eric and Woody with their songs.

'Oh no, he does very little. If a song's bad he'll say so and we'll do another. That's the kind of feeling we have, which is great because often people are afraid to say something's wrong.

'We've usually rehearsed the songs before we get intae the studio. This time we spent a week on our farm in Scotland. It was fantastic weather and we've got a courtyard, so we had the drums and everything outside. It was magic. When we've really rehearsed then perhaps Phil will say it needs an extra verse or something.'

What does Eric personally look for in a producer?

'Well, his job is to get the whole thing going, to make sure everything's in tune and tight. But I wanted somebody who we could be frank to and could also listen. Somebody we felt we could say, 'do you fancy doing this?' And I think in Phil why we've found that. That's why we're doing a second album with him. He's a nice guy. He knows what he's doing.

'He knows that we've been slagged off and he sympathises. And I think he's interested in us as musicians.'

Tell us something about your background, your home, your parents?

'I was a scruff! They kept threatening to expel me from school because I was always away. If we had gigs to do in the north of Scotland, I'd just disappear for four days.

'My Da (sic) was a blacksmith. No, he didnae shoe horses, he was a welder really. And my mother used to work. Money wasnae growing on trees, but it was all right.'

Eric left home and lived with his aunt in Edinburgh when he was 14, and as soon as he left school he moved into digs.

'I stayed in some right dives and most of the time I was hungry I'd go over to Alan and Derek's or Tam's for a meal... sob story! But it was good really.

'Staying in digs roughens you up and a lot of the time I had nothing to do but sit and write songs. And that's what I'm like. I could just go away and be alone for weeks. I like things happening and excitement but a lot of the time I just want to stroll off somewhere and play my guitar.' Pause.

'Sorry, I'm getting done up.' He hears a lead guitar in the studio. 'Woody's in there and he's doing my part.'

Eric has come across confidently but surprisingly lacking in big headed scenes. He's prepared to stand up for what he has achieved but he's not the type to boast. He is intense, but he ducks too close an examination of his emotions and his poise is impressive. He seems straightforward and candid. But then he falls headlong into a trap which I only half-heartedly spring for him.

'How old are you?' I ask.

'Nineteen, on October the 21st', he replies without hesitation.

I cast him a quizzical stare, hoping he will backtrack and tell the truth.

'Ta, ha, ha' he laughs nervously. 'It's true. But I don't feel 19 I feel 44', he continues brazenly. 'I know about things which you shouldn't know at our age. About being ripped off and conned and what have you.'

For a moment I'm tempted to challenge him, but his fib is a rather tragic, defenseless indication of the immense pressure he is under to achieve the impossible. To halt the march of time and stay caught in a time-warp, a Peter Pan, forever the teenager's teenage idol.

His manager, who later tells me that Eric is nearly 21, is almost obsessed with the idea that age and adult preoccupations will destroy the band's appeal.

'David Essex got married and look at him now,' he says. 'One of the boys in Pilot got married but he still talks about his 'bachelor flat' and I'm sure he's doing the right thing. There'll be plenty of time for the Rollers to do that in two years' time.'

Meanwhile, the only way, without being utterly cynical, for Eric to contend with the pretence of remaining immature, is to convince himself and others that he is really still a teenager. But it's still not easy. Dishonesty is essentially alien to his nature.

Surely, he misses the free adult life he must have led when he was still living in digs?

'What, the girls? Well, we've never been a band who dragged girls intae the back of the van. We always thought bands who did that were unprofessional. We've always basically been what we're said to be now. None of us are raving alcoholics or anything. That's not just publicity.'

Brief liaison on the road are one thing, but Eric doesn't seem to be allowed relationships of any kind with women.

'I know you think that we get orders and that we say 'yes, sir' and do everything we're told. But if we didnae want to do something we wouldnae do it. It's funny but it depends on what you want. If you feel you've got to do something bad enough you just give up certain things. I know it's hard to imagine but for ages we were on the road driving to gigs as far away from Edinburgh as Torquay. And, by the time you got home you were absolutely zonked anyway. All you wanted to do was sleep. Now it's even more difficult. The minute any one of us is seen with a girl it will be front page news.'

But he can't live exactly like a monk, can he?

'I don't know. Monks can be quite happy! I live the way I do out of choice and I think you'll find that whoever is best in their field is really dedicated.'

Is he resigned to his apparently celibate way of life?

'I was resigned to it four years ago,' he says loftily.

Oh, the rigours and vicissitudes of life at the top! The Rollers are obviously prepared for a minimum two years hard unremitting work to cash in on their mammoth success. Already their schedule is daunting. One day recently they flew to Germany at 7:30am, they were back in a Manchester TV studio by 7:30pm and they rounded off the evening recording their new album.

'It is hard,' says Eric, 'and you get tired. You start sleeping in for sessions and what have you. Our success has its disadvantages. The advantages are more. If it had never happened, we'd still be slogging it on the road.

'There are thousands of guys doing that and probably a lot of them deserve success more than we do, and there's not much we can do about it. But we can say that groups don't appear out of nowhere with a hit record. You don't get picked off the street and told 'right, sing this and sing that,' it never works like that. At least, if it does, then it won't last very long. Alan and Derek and Tam have been together for seven years, and a thing like that never ends overnight. It just goes too deep.'

Is Rollermania a dream for him or has he come to terms with the extent to which he is idolised?

'Yes and no. I don't think we see the half of it. We used to try and shop in Edinburgh but now it's impossible and you think 'Is this fuss really for us?'

'We see the mania side of it at concerts but most of the time we're in hotel bedrooms and we have our farm which is miles away from anywhere and so we're out of sight of the whole thing. We don't realise what's happening. None of us have friends outside the group. The six of us are stuck together. We're inside and IT's outside.

'The only time you realise the extent of it is when something happens like – well, I went up to Tam's house recently for tea. He made it and I began to drink and then I looked at the mug and my face was on it. That's when you begin to think. It's amazing?'

© Caroline Coon

Appendix 2

Timeline

1944	Duncan McIntosh Longmuir and Georgina Alice Burnie Sim, Alan's parents, are married in Edinburgh
1948	Alan Longmuir is born
1951	Derek Longmuir is born
1958	Alan sees Elvis in *Jailhouse Rock* at cinema
1963	Alan leaves school
1964	The Beatles play Edinburgh. Longmuir brothers witness Beatlemania.
	Longmuir brothers decide to form a band. They are joined by their cousin Neil Porteous.
	Alan begins plumbing apprenticeship
1965	Alan, Derek and Neil play publicly for first time in a talent contest at the bandstand on Princes Street Gardens, Edinburgh
	Nobby Clark joins band as vocalist. The band christen themselves The Saxons
	Dave Pettigrew joins the band on guitar
	The Saxons play their first paid gig at Cairns Church Hall
1966	Greig Ellison joins the group on guitar. Dave Pettigrew moves to keyboards
	Mike Ellison, Greig's brother, joins band as a second vocalist

1967   Tam Paton becomes manager

           The band decide to rename themselves the Bay City
           Rollers

           Mike Ellison leaves the band

           Neil Porteous leaves the band

           Rollers support The Bee Gees at Rosewell Miners'
           Institute

           Keith Norman joins the Rollers also on keyboards

1969   Alan Dunn joins

           Alan Dunn leaves

           Davie Paton recruited to Rollers on lead guitar

           Keith Norman leaves the band

           Billy Lyall joins the Rollers on keyboards

1970   Alan resigns his plumbing post and turns professional
           as a musician

           Eric Manclark joins the Rollers

           Neil Henderson joins the Rollers

1971   Billy Lyall leaves the Rollers

           Davie Paton leaves the Rollers

           Archie Marr joins the Rollers on keyboards

           Bay City Rollers sign to Bell Records

           Keep on Dancing is released and becomes the band's
           first hit

1972   *We Can Make Music* fails to chart

           Eric Manclark leaves the Rollers

           Neil Henderson leaves the Rollers

           John Devine joins the band on rhythm guitar

           Eric Faulkner joins the band on lead guitar

Archie Marr quits the group

Rollers win Luxembourg Grand Prix International contest

Manana is released and fails to chart

1973   *Saturday Night* is released and fails to chart

Nobby Clark leaves the band

Les McKeown replaces Nobby as lead vocalist

Remember is released as a single

1974   *Remember* becomes Rollers' second chart hit

John Devine leaves the band

Stuart 'Woody' Wood replaces him

Shang-A-Lang reaches number two in the chart

Alan's mother dies

Summerlove Sensation makes number three in the chart

The band's first album *Rollin'* makes number one in the chart

All of Me Loves All of You makes number four in the singles chart

Rollers embark on first national tour

1975   Band is voted Most Popular Group at the Carl Alan Awards; the award is presented by Princess Anne

Former band members Davie Paton and Billy Lyall make number one with their band Pilot and the song *January*

Bye Bye Baby becomes first number one single and the bestselling record of the year

Johnnie Walker refuses to play *Bye Bye Baby* on Radio One. He says it is 'garbage'

Shang-A-Lang TV series airs

After stepping in to help control some Rollers' fans, an off-duty policeman suffers a fatal heart attack

Fans invade the wedding of Alan's sister, Betty

Daily Express calls for Rollers' concerts to be banned

Second album *Once Upon a Star* reaches number one

Give a Little Love becomes Rollers' second number one single

Near riot at Mallory Park, Leicestershire, during Rollers' appearance sparks outrage

Alan purchases his dream home in Dollar, Scotland

Money Honey, the first single penned by Rollers' members, makes number 3 in the singles chart

London Weekend Television concert is beamed live into America. Fans riot and band members are injured

Third album *Wouldn't You Like It?* makes number three

1976   *Saturday Night* reaches number one in the US single charts

Band visit US on publicity tour and are met with hysteria

Alan leaves the band and is replaced by Ian Mitchell

Love Me Like I Love You makes number four in the UK charts

Rollers undertake national tour of US

1977   Alan releases first solo single *I'm Confessing*. It fails to chart in the UK

1978   Alan rejoins the Bay City Rollers after working on the *Strangers in the Wind* album. The album fails to chart in UK or US

Rollers move to US to make prime time TV series

	Alan celebrates 30th birthday in Hollywood
	Les McKeown leaves the Bay City Rollers
1979	Duncan Faure replaces Les McKeown
	Elevator album is released but fails to chart
	Alan sacks Tam Paton as band manager
	Legal routes to recovering band earnings begin
	Alan stars in South African film *Burning Rubber*
1981	*Ricochet* album is released but fails to chart
1982	Tam Paton imprisoned after being found guilty on underage sex charges
1984	Derek Longmuir retires from band and music
1985	Alan marries Jan
1986	Alan's son Jordan is born
	Alan and Jan buy the Castle Campbell Hotel in Dollar
1988	Alan's marriage disintegrates and the hotel goes bust
1989	Alan's dad dies
1990	Alan resumes his plumbing career while playing and touring intermittently with various versions of the Rollers
1994	Alan meets Eileen Rankin
1995	Alan suffers a heart attack
1997	Alan suffers a stroke
1998	Alan and Eileen marry
1999	Bay City Rollers reform and perform at the Millenium Hogmanay concert in Edinburgh
2003	*Bye Bye Baby* features in the hit film *Love Actually* sparking renewed interest in the Rollers
2009	Tam Paton dies

2010	Alan is made redundant from his job as a Byelaws Inspector
2014	Alan appears in Edinburgh Fringe show about his life *I Ran With The Gang*. The show is staged every year until Alan's death
2015	Bay City Rollers reform under the management of John McLaughlin. Concert tickets sell out in minutes
2016	Final Bay City Rollers concert
	Plaque to the band unveiled at Ryrie's in Haymarket area of Edinburgh. Alan and Derek attend
	A final settlement is reached with Sony over unpaid royalties from the record sales over the decades
2017	Alan makes guest appearances with Les McKeown's Legendary Bay City Rollers
2018	Alan begins work on his autobiography
	Alan dies after a short illness contracted whilst holidaying in Mexico
	Archie Marr dies following a house fire
	The planned run of *I Ran With The Gang* goes head with Derek Longmuir standing in for his brother
	Alan is buried in Bannockburn